Harnessing
Technology for
Deeper Learning

Scott McLeod
Julie Graber

Solution Tree | Press
a division of
Solution Tree

555 North Morton Street
Bloomington, IN 47404
800.733.6786 (toll free) / 812.336.7700
FAX: 812.336.7790

email: info@SolutionTree.com
SolutionTree.com

Visit **go.SolutionTree.com/technology** to download the free reproducibles in this book.

Printed in the United States of America

Library of Congress Cataloging-in-Publication Data

Names: McLeod, Scott, 1968- author. | Graber, Julie, 1969- author.
Title: Harnessing technology for deeper learning / Scott McLeod and Julie
   Graber.
Description: Bloomington, IN : Solution Tree Press, [2018] | Series:
   Solutions series | Includes bibliographical references.
Identifiers: LCCN 2018020649 | ISBN 9781943874088 (perfect bound)
Subjects: LCSH: Educational technology. | Education--Effect of technological
   innovations on. | Education--Aims and objectives.
Classification: LCC LB1028.3 .M3985 2018 | DDC 371.33--dc23 LC record available at
   https://lccn.loc.gov/2018020649

Solution Tree
Jeffrey C. Jones, CEO
Edmund M. Ackerman, President

Solution Tree Press
President and Publisher: Douglas M. Rife
Editorial Director: Sarah Payne-Mills
Art Director: Rian Anderson
Managing Production Editor: Kendra Slayton
Senior Editor: Amy Rubenstein
Developmental Editor: Miranda Addonizio
Proofreader: Ashante K. Thomas
Text Designer: Abigail Bowen
Cover Designer: Rian Anderson
Editorial Assistant: Sarah Ludwig

To Betsy, Isabel, Lucas, and Colin, who put up with my shenanigans and without whom everything would be meaningless.

—Scott

To Kendall, Erika, Austin, and Christian for encouraging me in all of my pursuits and inspiring me to follow my dreams. You are my world!

—Julie

Acknowledgments

Scott and Julie would like to thank the thousands of educators who have helped us pilot, revise, and refine the 4 Shifts Protocol. Although our names are on the cover, this book belongs to all of us.

Solution Tree Press would like to thank the following reviewers:

Amber Akapnitis
Supervising Teacher of Academic Services
Phoenix Day School for the Deaf
Phoenix, Arizona

Stacey Cool
Technology Integration Specialist
Merced Union High School District
Atwater, California

Beth Downing
Technology Coach
Granville Intermediate School
Granville, Ohio

Amy Kochensparger
Science Teacher
Eaton High School
Eaton, Ohio

Katherine Mulrooney
Language Arts Teacher
Immaculate Heart of Mary Catholic Elementary School
Wilmington, Delaware

David Olson
Social Studies Teacher
James Madison Memorial High School
Madison, Wisconsin

Visit **go.SolutionTree.com/technology** to download the free reproducibles in this book.

Table of Contents

About the Authors

 **Scott McLeod**, an associate professor of educational leadership at the University of Colorado Denver, is widely recognized as one of the United States' leading experts in preK–12 school technology leadership. He is the founding director of the University Council for Educational Administration's Center for the Advanced Study of Technology Leadership in Education (CASTLE), the only university center in the United States dedicated to the technology needs of school administrators. He is the co-creator of the *Did You Know? (Shift Happens)* video series and the 4 Shifts technology integration discussion protocol.

Scott has worked with hundreds of schools, districts, universities, and other organizations and has received numerous awards for his technology leadership work, including the 2016 Award for Outstanding Leadership from the International Society for Technology in Education (ISTE). In 2015, he was one of three finalists to be the director of the Iowa Department of Education. In 2011, he was a visiting faculty fellow at the University of Canterbury in New Zealand. Scott was one of the pivotal figures in Iowa's grassroots one-to-one computing movement, which has resulted in more than 220 school districts providing their students with powerful learning devices, and he founded the annual Iowa 1:1 Institute and EdCampIowa.

Scott blogs regularly about technology leadership and shares numerous resources through his Digital Leadership Daily SMS service, Twitter account, blog, and other information channels. Scott is a frequent keynote speaker and workshop facilitator at regional, state, national, and international conferences. He has written over 170 articles and other publications, coauthored the book *Different Schools for a Different World*, and coedited *What School Leaders Need to Know About Digital Technologies and Social Media*.

To learn more about Scott's work, visit his blog, *Dangerously Irrelevant* (http://dangerouslyirrelevant.org), or follow @mcleod on Twitter.

Julie Graber is an instructional technology consultant on a technology innovation team for Prairie Lakes Area Education Agency in Iowa where she supports educators with effective teaching, learning, leading, and technology practices. She is a passionate educator who is most interested in seeing teachers and administrators improve authentic learning opportunities for students. Her many areas of expertise include deeper thinking with technology, authentic learning, curriculum design, and performance tasks and assessments. Prior to Julie being a teaching, learning, and technology consultant, she spent thirteen years as a technology coordinator and business and computer teacher.

Julie is an Authentic Intellectual Work (AIW) coach and has coached elementary, middle, and high school teams of teachers on how to use the framework in order to increase the level of intellectual demand as well as the authenticity of the work that students are asked to do. She has served on several state leadership teams, including the North Central Science, Technology, Engineering, and Math (STEM) Hub Advisory Board and the Design Team for the Iowa Competency-Based Education Collaborative, and has provided guidance for schools to increase STEM education in their classrooms and move them toward competency-based and personalized learning. Julie is certified in the Instructional Practices Inventory and provides training for Defined STEM, a K–12 curriculum resource with engaging project-based lessons on real-world scenarios. Jay McTighe, author and speaker, asked Julie to join his consulting group, McTighe and Associates, to conduct workshops for educators using the Understanding by Design curriculum framework. Julie is the co-creator of the 4 Shifts discussion protocol and a regular local, state, and national presenter focusing on authentic work and student-centered, personalized and project-based learning.

To learn more about Julie's work, follow @jgraber on Twitter.

To book Scott McLeod or Julie Graber for professional development, contact pd@SolutionTree.com.

Foreword

By William M. Ferriter

Can I ask you a tough question? How many students in your classrooms are truly satisfied with the learning spaces you have created for them? If your students reflect the national average, the answer is bound to be discouraging. Fewer than four in ten high schoolers report being engaged in their classes, and students often list boredom as the primary reason for dropping out of school (Busteed, 2013). Over 70 percent of students who don't graduate report having lost interest by ninth grade and, worse yet, the majority of dropouts are convinced that motivation is all that prevented them from earning a diploma (Azzam, 2007).

These numbers are troubling for anyone passionate about schools. They indicate systemic failure on the part of practitioners to inspire learners and warn us of the immediate need to transform education—a warning that school leadership expert and series contributor Scott McLeod (2014) issues:

> If we truly care about preparing kids for life and work success—we need schools to be different. If economic success increasingly means moving away from routine cognitive work, schools need to also move in that direction. If our analog, ink-on-paper information landscapes outside of school have been superseded by environments that are digital and online and hyperconnected and mobile, our information landscapes inside of school also should reflect those shifts. If our students' extracurricular learning opportunities often are richer and deeper than what they experience in their formal educational settings, it is time for us to catch up.

Scott is right, isn't he? Our schools really do need to catch up if they are going to remain relevant in a world where learning is more important than schooling— and catching up can only start when we are willing to rethink everything. We need to push aside the current norms defining education—that teachers are to govern, direct, and evaluate student work; that mastering content detailed in predetermined curricula is the best indicator of student success; that assessment and remediation are more important than feedback and reflection; that the primary reason for investing in tools and technologies is to improve on existing practices.

It's time to implement notions that better reflect the complexity of the world in which we live.

That is the origin of this series. It is my attempt to give a handful of the most progressive educators that I know a forum for detailing what they believe it will take to *make schools different*. Each book encourages readers to question their core beliefs about what teaching and learning look like in action. More important, each title provides readers with practical steps and strategies for reimagining their day-to-day practices. Here's your challenge: no matter how unconventional ideas may seem at first, and no matter how uncomfortable they make you feel, find a way to take action. There is no other way to create the learning spaces that your students deserve.

Introduction
Framing the Challenge

Let's face it: most schools struggle with their technology integration efforts. They ardently believe that they need to utilize digital devices and online environments in their classrooms. They have attempted to invest in the digital tools that they think are necessary for student success in the 21st century. And yet most are failing to realize the hopes and dreams that accompanied their technological purchases. In almost every school, administrators, teachers, parents, and especially students will tell you that—with the exception of a few isolated pockets of innovation—digital technologies are not really transforming the learning experience.

Education researchers and commentators have noted for many years how most learning technologies lack impact. Stanford professor Larry Cuban (2001) chronicles his skepticism regarding digital learning tools in publications spanning a decade and a half, most famously in his book *Oversold and Underused: Computers in the Classroom*. He notes that educators continue to do the same things that they always have done in their classrooms, only with more expensive digital devices. Because teachers typically implement learning technologies as "add-ons to solve deep and abiding problems in . . . schools," they "remain a band-aid promising solutions to ill-framed problems" (Cuban, 2016).

The popular press and national news media are awash with headlines that echo this skepticism regarding the power of learning technologies. *The Atlantic*, for example, asks whether classrooms should ban smartphones (Barnwell, 2016). Similarly, a feature story in *The Washington Post* argues that smart students shouldn't use laptops in their classes (Guo, 2016). Writers and reporters for *The New York Times* (Richtel, 2010), PBS (Oppenheimer, 2010), and National Public Radio (Hamilton, 2008) all express concern about the negative impact of technology on our thinking, attempting to dispel the notion that humans can multitask. Andreas Schleicher, education director for the Organisation for Economic Co-operation and Development (OECD), states that technology "is doing more harm than good" (Bagshaw, 2016). Even Clay Shirky (2014), one of America's most noted internet experts, asks his students to put their laptops away during class, a request that Dan Rockmore (2014) echoes in *The New Yorker*.

Techno-skepticism isn't confined to the domain of education. Numerous technology critics routinely express their concern about the negative impacts of the digital world on our daily lives. For example, Andrew Keen's (2007) *The Cult of the Amateur* was an alleged "wake-up call" to the "freewheeling, narcissistic atmosphere that pervades the Web" (back cover). Mark Bauerlein (2008), author of *The Dumbest Generation*, states that the digital age is stupefying young Americans and jeopardizing our future. Technologist Jaron Lanier (2010) argues that technology is shaping us rather than the other way around. Michael Bugeja (2005) claims that *interpersonal divides* occur when people spend too much time in virtual rather than "real" communities. Sherry Turkle (2011) contends that our relentless digital connection is actually leading to new forms of solitude. Nicholas Carr (2010) posits that the internet is eroding our ability to engage in deep and creative thought. These examples only scratch the surface; the list is seemingly endless. Humans are adept at manufacturing anxieties and fears—both real and perceived—whenever seismic changes are afoot.

And yet, despite all of the anxious hand-wringing and reflexive teeth-gnashing, most of us also seem to understand quite deeply that these new digital tools and environments bring us great power. If they didn't, they wouldn't have pervaded our homes and offices so quickly. They wouldn't have infiltrated our attention and our energy and our enthusiasm. There must be something there, right?

The Benefits of Technology

Of course there is. We now have the ability to communicate almost instantaneously with people all over the planet. We can learn anytime, anywhere, from anyone, about anything we want. We are able to create content, reach others, and collaborate in ways that were previously unimaginable to noncorporate or nongovernment entities. We can access almost all of human knowledge through the small mobile devices that we carry in our pockets and purses. The power that we have as learners and teachers these days would have been inconceivable to our ancestors just a couple of generations ago. To say that mobile phones, laptops, tablets, apps, virtual and augmented reality, interactive games and simulations, adaptive learning systems, online websites, multimedia feeds, and other digital environments have little to no place in education is ludicrous. There is no better way to cement schools' irrelevance than to ignore the digital transformations that are reshaping the rest of society.

The key, then, is to figure out how to use these digital tools and to use them well. Instead of arguing that they should be banned or kept from our students, educators and parents should be determining how students should use them and for what purposes. Our thoughtful intentionality can shape our students' learning in positive ways. If the primary criticism of technology integration is that schools will continue to see limited impacts from their digital learning investments until they change, then the solution is to rethink learning and teaching and schooling, not to ignore or ban our powerful technologies.

About This Book

In this book, we describe our approach to this challenge and model how we are working with teachers, administrators, instructional coaches, and technology integrationists to transform digital learning opportunities for students. The main driver of our efforts, and this book, is the 4 Shifts Protocol, a discussion tool that we developed to help educators better integrate technology into their classrooms.

Chapter 1 offers a review of current frameworks and their advantages and disadvantages. In chapter 2, we introduce the 4 Shifts Protocol as a potential solution to the complex challenges of classroom technology integration. The next two chapters illustrate how to use the 4 Shifts Protocol to redesign lessons and units for elementary schools (chapter 3) and middle and high schools (chapter 4). Chapter 5 provides two examples of how to design lessons and units from scratch using the protocol. In chapter 6, we conclude with valuable tips and strategies for using the 4 Shifts Protocol and close with an epilogue that invites you, the reader, to engage with us further.

Chapter 1
Seeking a New Approach

The ongoing criticisms of educators' current technology integration practices are deadly accurate. Although most schools have a lot of technology, they rarely use it well. As a result, they usually find that their technology-related efforts aren't paying off as they had hoped, leaving them open to understandable and easily anticipated questions about time, energy, and financial cost. There is a *lot* of replicative use—doing the same things that educators used to do in analog classrooms, only with more expensive tools—and many schools and educators are using technology simply for technology's sake. Until schools can get beyond basic replication with the digital devices that they've purchased, they are never going to satisfy the questions and concerns of their parents, communities, and outside critics.

Educators need better resources in order to move toward more transformative technology environments in which students and teachers use digital tools to actually do things that they couldn't previously do in analog learning spaces. In this chapter, we review several conceptual models that are worth understanding, but they also are insufficient for most school systems.

Current Frameworks

Instructional technology professors in colleges and universities primarily use the Technological Pedagogical Content Knowledge (TPACK) framework (figure 1.1, page 6).

TPACK evolved from professor Lee Shulman's (1986, 1987) work regarding *pedagogical content knowledge* which, in a nutshell, says that effective teachers live at the intersection of content knowledge (CK) and pedagogical knowledge (PK).

5

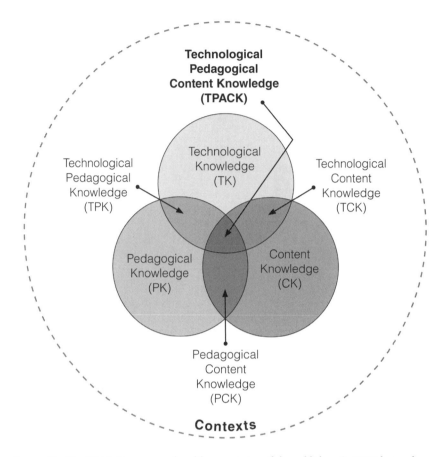

Source: Koehler, 2012. Image reproduced by permission of the publisher, © 2012 by tpack.org.

Figure 1.1: Technological Pedagogical Content Knowledge framework.

In other words, they know their stuff, can teach it well, and understand how to live at the nexus of those two domains.

Punya Mishra and Matthew J. Koehler (2006) add a third domain to Shulman's framework: technological knowledge (TK). They posit that technology tools are separate from both content and traditional pedagogy and add a new dimension to classroom teaching that is worth mastering. Digital learning tools require teachers to consider new content and pedagogy intersections as they pull those tools into their day-to-day instruction. That made sense to most people, and instructional technology faculty have been conducting research using the TPACK framework ever since (see for example Archambault & Barnett, 2016; Kessler et al., 2017).

Although TPACK is the darling of the postsecondary crowd, the Substitution Augmentation Modification Redefinition (SAMR) framework (Puentedura, 2006) is dominant in most elementary and secondary schools. The SAMR framework looks like a ladder with four rungs. Substitution sits at the bottom with Augmentation and then Modification above it. Redefinition is at the top. The definitions of each are as follows.

- **Substitution:** Technology acts as a direct tool substitute, with no functional change.

- **Augmentation:** Technology acts as a direct tool substitute, with functional improvement.

- **Modification:** Technology allows for significant task redesign.

- **Redefinition:** Technology allows for the creation of new tasks, previously inconceivable.

The lower two rungs illustrate how technology can *enhance* our work while the upper two rungs depict how technology can *transform* our work. The basic idea of SAMR is that, over time, our technology integration efforts should move beyond substitution (that is, replication, or doing the same things we did in analog environments) and toward redefinition (that is, transformation, or doing things differently than we could in analog environments). That's an easy idea to understand—and a worthy goal—and educators have been trying for years now to integrate SAMR into their technology integration thinking and professional development.

The Replacement, Amplification, and Transformation (RAT) framework appeared in 2006 a few months before SAMR. Joan Hughes, Ruth Thomas, and Cassandra Scharber (2006) postulate three categories that preservice teachers could use to increase their critical decision-making regarding technology integration. The RAT framework is similar to the SAMR framework but collapses SAMR's middle two categories (augmentation and modification) into one (amplification). Here are some basic definitions for each category.

- **Replacement:** Technology serves as a different (digital) means to the same instructional practices.

- **Amplification:** Technology increases efficiency, effectiveness, and productivity of the same instructional practices.

- **Transformation:** Technology invents new instruction, learning, or curricula.

Again, the idea is that we want students and teachers to get beyond Replacement-level technology integration (that is, replication) and move toward Transformation, at least in some of their learning and teaching practices.

The Arizona and Florida Technology Integration Matrices (Arizona K12 Center, 2012; Florida Center for Instructional Technology, 2011) take a slightly different approach. Both models place technology integration within the context of categories of use. For instance, both models say that technology usage should be active, collaborative, constructive, authentic, and goal directed. Here are the definitions from the Florida matrix.

- **Active:** Students are actively engaged in using technology as a tool rather than passively receiving information from the technology.

- **Collaborative:** Students use technology tools to collaborate with others rather than working individually at all times.

- **Constructive:** Students use technology tools to connect new information to their prior knowledge rather than to passively receive information.

- **Authentic:** Students use technology tools to link learning activities to the world beyond the instructional setting rather than working on decontextualized assignments.

- **Goal directed:** Students use technology tools to set goals, plan activities, monitor progress, and evaluate results rather than simply completing assignments without reflection.

For each of the five definitions, teachers can be at five different levels of technology integration: (1) Entry, (2) Adoption, (3) Adaptation, (4) Infusion, or (5) Transformation. These five levels are similar to the SAMR framework's four levels or the RAT framework's three levels. The matrices help a teacher understand that her technology integration for a given activity may be strong in one area (for example, active technology use) while simultaneously low in another (for example, authentic technology use).

All of these frameworks are useful as basic mental models. We like the idea embedded in nearly all of them that teachers should be moving toward transformation rather than replication, which addresses the primary concerns of Cuban (2016) and many others (for example, Bauerlein, 2008; Carr, 2010; Schleicher, cited in Bagshaw, 2016). We like the fact that the RAT framework collapses the often-confusing middle two categories of SAMR (Augmentation and Modification) into one simple category (Amplification). We like Florida's and Arizona's understanding that educators can be at differing levels—even for the same technology-infused activity—depending on which outcomes we're examining (Arizona K12 Center, 2012; Florida Center for Instructional Technology, 2011). And we like TPACK's emphasis on integrating and thinking about the intersections of all three of the domains of content, pedagogy, and technology. All of this makes sense to us.

What we have found to be difficult, however, is implementing these frameworks in practice. While they are useful mental models, *they don't usually help educators know what to do differently.* Take SAMR, for instance. If a mentor or outside observer says to a teacher, "You know, I think that lesson you just facilitated is at the Augmentation level and you should try to move it toward Redefinition," the framework doesn't help that teacher very much in knowing what to change instructionally, particularly since SAMR is a technology usage continuum, not a learning continuum (that is, an instructional activity can be high on the SAMR continuum but still be low-level learning). Similarly, without a whole lot of analysis and conversation—the quality of which will be highly variable across schools and districts—it is usually fairly difficult for teachers to recognize in which TPACK intersections their technology integration practices may be (and, probably more importantly, in which intersections they're not).

Limitations of Current Frameworks

In our work with classroom teachers, we have noticed that they find many of these frameworks to be judgmental in the sense that they feel inferior or criticized if their technology integration is not frequently or always at the transformation level. They feel explicit pressure from instructional technology coaches or administrators to move toward transformation—which is indeed necessary in many instances—but these leaders accompany it with very little guidance on what to do differently in order to make desired shifts happen. In other words, if teachers already knew what to change, most of them probably would be doing it already. The overlay of a framework that teachers see as vague but judgmental doesn't make the task instructionally easier and frequently makes it psychologically harder. Exhortations to do something different or better don't help teachers if they don't have the know-how to do so.

Finally, and probably most important, the shorthand definitions that accompany each element within the frameworks aren't sufficiently clear to identify where in the frameworks educators should situate a particular lesson, unit, or activity. The middle two levels of SAMR are often muddled, for example, and a quick internet search will illustrate that people have wildly divergent beliefs about how they interpret SAMR; they equate it with Bloom's taxonomy (Bloom, Engelhart, Furst, Hill, & Krathwohl, 1956), a swimming pool, types of coffee, moving from a canoe to a submarine, and other metaphors. In our own workshops, we have witnessed several different groups of technology integrationists place the same technology-infused lesson into all four of the SAMR levels. Technology integrationists are supposed to be experts in this area, both familiar with the SAMR framework and tasked with implementing it within their schools and districts. And even they can't agree on where to place a lesson. While the value may be in the discussion rather than in the exact placement of the learning and teaching activity, we are very empathetic toward more novice teachers who often feel frustrated and defeated as they struggle to find meaning, make sense of the frameworks, and improve their practice.

The challenge with all of these models and frameworks is that they're just that: models and frameworks. They're big-picture, conceptual depictions of how we should be thinking about how the world works. They are not intended to give more explicit guidance about what to change. While some of these frameworks have subsequent supporting documentation or resources that help with aspects of this (see for example the TPACK learning activity types from Harris & Hofer, 2009), these resources often exist behind publisher paywalls, making them more difficult for teachers to access. We take a different approach, one that we explain in the next chapter.

Chapter 2
Introducing the
4 Shifts Protocol

The frameworks we describe in the previous chapter are helpful as general overviews of what schools are trying to accomplish with classroom technology integration. But we still felt that we needed more. We wanted to have different and more detailed—but still structured—conversations with the teachers and administrators whom we serve and we just felt that existing models were too vague and general. So we went on a hunt for something more specific. Our goal was to find a discussion protocol, classroom observation template, conversation tool, or *something* that allows educators to concretely and explicitly assess technology integration within the context of higher-order-thinking skills that are steeped in important disciplinary concepts. We found very quickly that what we were looking for didn't seem to exist.

The Search for the Ideal Approach

The list of possibilities we researched was long: Bloom's revised taxonomy (Bloom et al., 1956; Krathwohl, 2002); Webb's (2002) Depth of Knowledge; Richard Stiggins' target types (Stiggins, Arter, Chappuis, & Chappuis, 2012); the Instructional Practices Inventory (Valentine, 2018); Authentic Intellectual Work (Center for Authentic Intellectual Work, 2018); Tony Wagner's (2008) seven survival skills; Iowa's characteristics of effective instruction (Iowa Core, 2018); the generally agreed-on four Cs of critical thinking, creativity, communication, and collaboration (Partnership for 21st Century Learning, 2017); TPACK (Mishra & Koehler, 2006); SAMR (Puentedura, 2006); RAT (Hughes et al., 2006); the Technology and Learning Spectrum (Porter, 2010); the Florida and Arizona

Technology Integration Matrices (Arizona K12 Center, 2012; Florida Center for Instructional Technology, 2011); the universal constructs, cognitive complexity documents, and 21st century technology literacy concepts and skills in the Iowa Core (Iowa Core, 2010); Barbara Bray and Kathleen McClaskey's (2014) personalization versus individualization versus differentiation chart; the International Society for Technology and Education (ISTE, 2018b) technology standards for students and teachers; the Partnership for 21st Century Learning (2018) framework; Grant Wiggins and Jay McTighe's work regarding Understanding by Design (Wiggins & McTighe, 2005) and essential questions (McTighe & Wiggins, 2013); the National Council of Teachers of English (2017) 21st century literacies framework; and many, many more.

Each framework, document, instrument, or set of standards has a piece of what we wanted but none of them contain the entirety. For instance, we like the IPI's emphasis on higher-order-thinking skills and on who's doing the work and how, but it has little depth regarding technology integration, even when we look at the technology version of the protocol (the IPI-T; Valentine, 2018). Likewise, we realized very quickly that a lesson could be high on the SAMR levels but still have students engaged in low-level factual recall and procedural regurgitation. Wagner's (2008) seven survival skills and the technology integration matrices emphasize many of the elements that we are looking for but de-emphasize other critical components such as metacognition and reflection or communication, respectively. Bray and McClaskey's (2014) chart does a great job of focusing on student agency and inquiry but is less robust when it comes to technology or authentic work. And so on . . . .

The 4 Shifts Protocol

Lacking a comprehensive protocol, we decided to make one ourselves. Because we are acutely interested in changing technology-infused instruction to be deeper and more robust, the 4 Shifts Protocol[1] takes a different and very hands-on approach. Instead of trying to come up with an overarching grand theory of action, the protocol instead attempts to get at some specific, concrete look-fors and think-abouts that can help teachers contemplate what instructional changes they might make in their units, lessons, or activities. Rather than a unifying conceptual framework, the protocol is meant to be a down-in-the-weeds (re)design resource.

We organized the *4 Shifts Protocol* according to the four big shifts that we see schools moving toward: (1) deeper thinking and learning, (2) authentic work,

---

[1] We called previous versions of the 4 Shifts Protocol the Technology-Rich Unit Design and Classroom Observation Template (trudacot).

(3) student agency and personalization, and (4) technology infusion. These shifts are the foundation of successful technology integration in the classroom. The current version of the protocol appears here in figure 2.1 and you can visit http://bit .ly/4shifts for more 4 Shifts Protocol resources.

A. Deeper Thinking and Learning. Deeper learning schools are moving from an overwhelming emphasis on students mostly doing lower-level thinking tasks—factual recall and procedural regurgitation—to students more often engaging in tasks of greater cognitive complexity—creativity, critical thinking, problem solving, and effective communication and collaboration. In other words, students are living more often on the upper levels of Bloom's taxonomy (or Webb's Depth of Knowledge) than the lower ones.

Domain Knowledge. Is student work deeply rooted in discipline-specific and -relevant knowledge, skills, and dispositions?

    Yes   No   Somewhat

    Deeper Learning. If yes, is student work focused around big, important themes and concepts[1] that are central to the discipline rather than isolated topics, trivia, or minutiae?

        Yes   No   Somewhat

[1] Do student learning activities and assessments go beyond low-level facts and procedures? Are students just regurgitating syntheses and analyses provided by an information source or the teacher?

Critical Thinking. Do learning activities and assessments allow students to engage in deep critical thinking and analysis?

    Yes   No   Somewhat

Problem Solving. Do learning activities and assessments allow students to engage in complex and messy (not simple) problem solving?

    Yes   No   Somewhat

Creativity. Do students have the opportunity to design, create, make, or otherwise add value that is unique to them?

    Yes   No   Somewhat

Figure 2.1: The 4 Shifts Protocol. continued →

*Visit **go.SolutionTree.com/technology** for a free reproducible version of this figure.*

Metacognition. Do students have the opportunity to reflect on their planning, thinking, work, and progress?

>   Yes   No   Somewhat

>   If yes, can students identify what they're learning, not just what they're doing?

>   Yes   No   Somewhat

Assessment Alignment. Are all assessments aligned cognitively[2] with standards, learning goals, instruction, and learning activities?

>   Yes   No   Somewhat

_____

[2] Standards and learning goals drive everything, including depth of student thinking and the necessary accompanying assessments. Assessments should be aligned to the cognitive complexity asked of students.

B. Authentic Work. Deeper learning schools are moving from isolated, siloed academic work to environments that provide students more opportunities to engage with and contribute to relevant local, national, and international interdisciplinary communities. Students begin fostering active networks with individuals and organizations for mutual benefit.

Real or Fake. Is student work authentic and reflective of that done by experts outside of school?

>   Yes   No   Somewhat

Authentic Role. Are students asked to take on an authentic societal role as part of their learning?

>   Yes   No   Somewhat

Domain Practices. Are students utilizing authentic, discipline-specific practices and processes?[3]

>   Yes   No   Somewhat

_____

[3] Engaging in the actual practices and processes that people in that discipline use; for example, doing what historians, scientists, writers, artists, business professionals, and others do, not some artificial or classroom version of that work

Domain Technologies. Are students utilizing authentic, discipline-specific tools and technologies?[4]

Yes   No   Somewhat

---

[4] Using the actual tools and technologies that people in that discipline use; for example, using the real tools that historians, scientists, writers, artists, business professionals, and others use, not some artificial or classroom versions of those tools

Research and Information Literacy Strategies. Are students utilizing authentic, discipline-specific research, inquiry, and information literacy strategies?

Yes   No   Somewhat

Authentic Assessment. Are students creating real-world products or performances for authentic audiences?

Yes   No   Somewhat

Contribution. If yes, does student work make a contribution to an audience beyond the classroom walls to the outside world?

Yes   No   Somewhat

Assessment Technology. Are digital technologies being used in authentic ways to facilitate the assessment process?

Yes   No   Somewhat

C. Student Agency and Personalization. Deeper learning schools are moving from classrooms that are overwhelmingly teacher controlled to learning environments that enable greater student agency—ownership and control of what, how, when, where, who with, and why they learn. Student agency allows for greater personalization, individualization, and differentiation of the learning process.

Learning Goals. Who selected what is being learned?

Students   Teachers   Both

Learning Activity. Who selected how it is being learned?

Students   Teachers   Both

Assessment of Learning. Who selected how students demonstrate their knowledge and skills and how that will be assessed?

Students   Teachers   Both

continued →

Talk Time. During the lesson or unit, who is the primary driver of the talk time?[5]

> Students   Teachers   Both

---

[5] Who's doing most of the talking, determining who can talk and when they can talk?

Work Time. During the lesson or unit, who is the primary driver of the work time?[6]

> Students   Teachers   Both

---

[6] Who's making the decisions about the work time and ensuring progress?

Interest-Based. Is student work reflective of their interests or passions?

> Yes   No   Somewhat

Initiative. Do students have the opportunity to initiate, be entrepreneurial, be self-directed, and go beyond the given parameters of the learning task or environment?

> Yes   No   Somewhat

Technology Selection. Who selected which technologies are being used?

> Students   Teachers   Both

Technology Usage. Who is the primary user of the technology?

> Students   Teachers   Both

D. Technology Infusion. Deeper learning schools are moving from local classrooms that are largely based on pens and pencils, notebook paper, ring binders, and printed textbooks to globally connected learning spaces that are deeply and richly infused with technology. The new affordances of mobile computing devices and online environments allow the first three shifts mentioned here to move into high gear.

Communication. How are students communicating?

> Alone[7]   In pairs   In triads   In groups larger than three
>
> If with others, with whom? (circle all that apply)
>
> > Students in this school   Students in another school
> > Adults in this school   Adults outside of this school

---

[7] Working in isolation (no communication with others) or perhaps just communicating with the teacher (for example, call and response)

Communication Technologies. Are digital technologies being used to facilitate the communication processes?

>   Yes   No

>   If yes, in which ways? (circle all that apply)

>>   Writing   Photos and images   Charts and graphs
>>   Infographics   Audio   Video   Multimedia   Transmedia

Collaboration. How are students working?

>   Alone[8]   In pairs   In triads   In groups larger than three

>   If with others, with whom? (circle all that apply)

>>   Students in this school   Students in another school
>>   Adults in this school   Adults outside of this school

>   If with others, who is managing collaborative processes (planning, management, and monitoring)?

>>   Students   Teachers   Both

---

[8] Working in isolation (no communication with others) or perhaps just communicating with the teacher (for example, call and response)

Collaboration Technologies. Are digital technologies being used to facilitate collaborative processes?

>   Yes   No   Somewhat

>   If yes, in which ways? (circle all that apply)

>>   Online office suites   Email   Texting   Wikis   Blogs
>>   Videoconferencing   Mind mapping   Curation tools
>>   Project planning tools   Other

Technology Adds Value. Does technology add value so that students can do their work in better or different ways than are possible without the technology?

>   Yes   No   Somewhat

Technology as Means, Not End. When digital technologies are utilized, do the tools overshadow, mask, or otherwise draw the focus away from important learning?

>   Yes   No   Somewhat

continued →

Digital Citizenship. Are digital technologies utilized by students in both appropriate and empowering ways?[9]

Yes   No   Somewhat

---

[9] Effective digital citizenship conversations focus on both safe, responsible use *and* empowering, participating use. Digital citizenship discussions ideally are natural extensions of and accompaniments to students' ongoing, technology-enabled work rather than separate conversations or curricula.

We created the protocol to help us have the kinds of conversations with educators that we think are so desperately needed. In order to accomplish our instructional and conversational goals, we decided to focus on *instructional purpose*. When educators use digital technologies for learning and teaching, those uses should be intentional and targeted. Educators should be able to clearly articulate what technology infusion is intended to accomplish for them and their students. In other words, as thoughtful users of learning technologies, we all should continually ask the question, "Technology for the purpose of *what*?" The protocol's questions allow educators to think critically—and purposefully—about their technology integration.

When we work with educators on their instructional activities, we first identify the desired instructional purposes, which allows us to focus on just a section or two from the discussion protocol. We then know what questions to start asking about what teachers have designed and implemented in the classroom. For example, if a class activity pulls in learning technologies for the purposes of enhancing student choice and enabling greater *student agency and personalization* (section C of the protocol), we can ask questions about aspects of the lesson such as who is setting learning goals and who is the primary user of the technology in order to see whether teachers are accomplishing their desired purposes. Similarly, if teachers select classroom technologies with the intent of enabling students to do more *authentic work* (Section B of the protocol), we can ask questions regarding the use of domain-specific practices and processes and whether students are creating real-world products or performances for authentic audiences.

The most powerful uses of the protocol occur when administrators and teachers get beyond merely answering the questions in a particular section and instead begin using the questions to help them frame their instructional redesign work. For instance, when a principal or teaching peer asks an educator, "What if you wanted the answer to this question to be 'yes' instead of 'no'?" or "What if you wanted the answer to this question to be 'the student' instead of 'the teacher'? How could we get there?," those questions can spark powerful conversations that shift teachers' conceptions about instructional depth and robust technology usage.

In other words, we are attempting with the protocol to make very explicit the kinds of questions that we might ask during an instructional coaching conversation about which intersection of TPACK—or level of SAMR—a particular instance of technology integration may be inhabiting (and how to shift it toward greater robustness). We are attempting with the protocol to put some structure around the very basic question, What are we trying to accomplish? If we're achieving those goals—as indicated by desired answers on the protocol—then awesome, let's pat ourselves on the back and keep doing that! But if not, we can use some of the protocol questions as design or redesign pivot points to shift the instructional activity in the directions we want.

In the chapters that follow, we include numerous examples of how teachers might use the 4 Shifts Protocol across a variety of subject areas and grade levels to design or redesign existing lessons, units, and instructional activities. Since we know of few books that have taken on the challenge of explicitly modeling lesson and unit redesign for deeper learning, we are attempting to help close that gap with the following scenarios. As you read through the examples, try to get a sense of how you might start using the protocol for your own instructional redesign work toward deeper thinking and learning, authentic work, student agency and personalization, and technology infusion. We have found that using the 4 Shifts Protocol with educators to redesign technology-infused lessons and units can be both instructionally powerful and professionally energizing. We hope that you do too.

Chapter 3
Redesigning Elementary School Lessons and Units

In this chapter, we present three examples to introduce you to the protocol and how you might use it for elementary lesson redesign. Chapters 4 and 5 include three secondary lesson redesign examples and two lessons—one elementary and one secondary—that we design from the beginning with the protocol. We encourage you to read through all of the examples, even if they're not in your grade level or subject area, to see what ideas may transfer into your own instructional work.

Elementary School Social Studies

Let's start our lesson redesign examples by taking a deeper look at Mystery Skype, an increasingly popular activity in elementary classrooms. Say that two teachers want to briefly connect their classrooms. These teachers may already know each other, have connected via social media, or have used an online classroom connection or brokerage site such as Skype in the Classroom (https://bit.ly/2ck6fgE; Microsoft, 2018). The two teachers know where in the world the other's classroom is but their students do not.

Mystery Skype

At a mutually agreed-on date and time, two teachers connect their classes using a videoconferencing tool such as Skype, Google Hangouts, or Zoom. Before the class-to-class interaction begins, the teachers assign students specific responsibilities, including roles like greeters, researchers, logical reasoners, questioners, and timekeepers. The ultimate goal of the Mystery Skype activity is to be the first class to guess the other's location by asking yes-or-no questions.

During their time together, each class takes turns asking yes-or-no questions of the other (for example, "Is your school close to a river?" or "Is it cold there?"). Once each class has identified the other's location correctly, all of the students celebrate, wave goodbye to each other, and disconnect the webcam. Most classes also then debrief how the activity went so that they can improve their questions for next time.

The Redesign

Mystery Skype has a lot of positives. Students who participate typically have a lot of fun, take their roles and responsibilities seriously, and use some technology tools to help with their research. Teachers like the differentiated roles for various student interests or skill sets. Additionally, they like that most students are actively engaged in and enthusiastic about the activity. They also say that Mystery Skype builds teamwork, fosters positive interdependence, and enhances students' critical thinking and global awareness. At first glance it might seem like this is a great use of classroom technology. Using the 4 Shifts Protocol (page 13), however, we can take a critical look at the activity and consider some redesign possibilities that alleviate some potential concerns.

The biggest limitation of Mystery Skype is that a class typically spends forty to fifty minutes in the activity but the primary (and, in our minds, meager) learning outcome is just to guess the location of some other class somewhere. Since learning time is precious and scarce—and sometimes teachers do multiple Mystery Skype activities per year—we can ask whether guessing someone's location is a substantive enough learning outcome to warrant the time. Yes, outcomes such as collaboration, teamwork, and speaking and listening skills are important, but maybe we also can achieve some more significant and cognitively complex outcomes on the content side.

Take a look at some questions from the 4 Shifts Protocol and imagine how we might redesign this activity around them.

- *Is student work focused around big, important themes and concepts that are central to the discipline rather than isolated topics, trivia, or minutiae?* (section A, page 13)

  - Currently it is not, but it could be if we allow the students to go beyond yes-or-no questions and simple location guessing. For instance, we could learn most of our history unit about the Middle East through activities created by and conversations with students from the Middle East (and they could learn about our region from us). Students on both sides would achieve a much more substantive understanding of their global peers' context and community. Similarly, we could view our online connection as an opportunity for students to construct knowledge around one of the five themes of geography, such as *region*. Students could generate questions regarding religions, political divisions, language, vegetation, and other regional differences. Once they have collected this information from their partner classroom, the students could use it to determine the particular region of the world in which the partner class is located and then explain the region in rich detail to others. Coordinating other online conversations with classes around the nation and world could help uncover the other four themes of geography as well (location, place, human-environment interaction, and movement).

- *Do learning activities and assessments allow students to engage in complex and messy (not simple) problem solving?* (section A)

    - Currently they do not, but they could if we allow the students to interact multiple times over several weeks with their global peers around local manifestations of larger, important global issues. For instance, we could set up five or six cross-classroom problem-solving teams—each of which collaborate using Google Docs and regular webcam meetings—around issues related to immigration, women's rights, or increasing the percentage of people in their community who vote.

- *When digital technologies are utilized, do the tools overshadow, mask, or otherwise draw the focus away from important learning?* (section D, page 17)

    - Yes, right now they absolutely do this. Although we see students using the webcam, and they're excited about the activity, the level of cognitive demand for this block of instructional time is pretty low, particularly for those students in peripheral roles who don't actually get to devise any of the questions to the other class. We can't let student enthusiasm and a little technology mask the underlying lack of learning complexity. Let's give them something more meaningful to work on together!

If we consider the protocol questions for the original activity, we think it is difficult to argue that Mystery Skype helps students learn important content. As a principal once said to us, "How is this any different from me holding an index card to my head and saying, 'Okay, we're playing *20 Questions*. Guess the location on this card.' Would we be okay with teachers spending multiple fifty-minute class periods on that?'" We can easily think of ways to reconfigure this activity so students are thinking and working at higher levels without sacrificing the other soft-skill benefits that don't relate to content such as student enthusiasm, cooperative teamwork, positive interdependence, and the connection to peers across the globe.

We frequently begin our conversations about technology-infused lesson redesign with Mystery Skype because it allows us to discuss with educators the concept of claims and evidence. For instance, if teachers claim that Mystery Skype fosters students' global awareness, we can ask them what evidence supports that since the only real interactions that students have with their peers elsewhere are a few yes-and-no questions (and answers) and some visual clues from the other classroom. That doesn't seem like much global awareness to us compared to other, richer possibilities. Similarly, if principals or instructional coaches claim that Mystery Skype fosters students' critical-thinking and problem-solving skills, we can ask them what evidence supports that since guessing the location is a pretty simple, noncomplex problem to solve and since at best only some of the designated student roles require critical thinking.

Some teachers do several—or even dozens—of one-and-done Mystery Skype activities per year. That's a lot of location guessing and a lot of time for an activity that doesn't have much academic content payoff, particularly in this era of increased school accountability mandates. By using some of the concrete look-fors and think-abouts in the 4 Shifts Protocol to help redesign the interactions, we can do much better than a one-time event in which students only get to ask yes-or-no questions and have little to no follow-up interaction with the other classes. When we originally ask teachers and principals what they think of Mystery Skype, nearly all of them say that they like the activity. After all, students' energy is high and they use some technology. But when we identify the activity's limitations, ask educators to redesign around the two ideas of deeper learning and student collaboration, and give them permission to walk away from the "guess the location" format, they always come up with great ideas that make the class-to-class interaction deeper, better, and more robust.

Elementary School English Language Arts

For our second example of instructional redesign, we look at a lesson that might happen in a North American classroom in October. The idea is to use the seasonal theme of pumpkins to engage students in books they are reading.

Pumpkin Book Report

In this lesson, fourth-grade students each choose a book for a book report and then decorate pumpkins to look like characters from their books. The teacher then uses the Flipsnack software program to make virtual flip books and display all of the videos that the students record about their character's name while they hold their pumpkin. The class gets to view the final Flipsnack show when it is done.

The Redesign

As we look at this lesson, we like the idea of trying to incorporate an interesting way for students to share information about the book they read. We also like that teachers allow students to read a book of their choosing. Finally, we thought that it was fun for the fourth graders to record themselves and then have all of the videos compiled together into one show using Flipsnack so that students and their parents can see what everyone else did.

In our minds, however, the fun of designing the pumpkin to look like a character in the book seems to have overshadowed the lack of a substantial learning goal. In fact, finding some substantive learning for the students in this project would be a good place to start. When we think of important fourth-grade English language arts (ELA) learning goals, we initially think of students having to describe a character by drawing on specific details in the text, such as character traits. In a redesigned version of this activity, instead of just stating the book character's name on video, students could tell why they chose that particular character and then describe the traits of that character. They could provide evidence of their character's traits by articulating text from the book that supports their interpretation. In addition to character traits, students could determine the theme of the story from details in the text, and they could create an image that depicts the major events of the story. By adding these ELA learning goals, teachers are asking students to think at a deeper level. As we amp up this revision, we also can address at a much higher level additional ELA learning goals in the areas of speaking and listening. Students now are telling at least part of a story using appropriate facts and relevant, descriptive details to support a theme while speaking clearly at an understandable pace. Students also could add audio and video recordings and visual displays to their presentations to enhance the development of the theme.

Even though students are sharing their work with their classmates, we think a key shift would be to have the students use technology to publish their work to a broader audience, one that is outside the classroom walls. Since in this instance the class already has a Facebook page, and the teacher also sends out a weekly parent newsletter, we think that embedding Flipsnack into these two communication tools for others to view helps increase the visibility of student work. By moving the end product outside of the classroom walls, the teacher also may find that students' concern about the quality of their work ratchets up since there now is a more authentic audience than just the teacher and classmates.

Even though we now have connected the lesson to some important, more substantive ELA learning goals and increased the depth of thinking, the beauty of this redesign is that we didn't sacrifice the fun parts of the lesson. Students still get to design a pumpkin like their character and display their videos in a Flipsnack show. We believe that teachers can achieve fun, technology, deeper thinking, and learning goals by slightly modifying the activity. With these changes, the lesson now reads something like this:

> During the month of October, fourth-grade students choose a book for a video book report. They then select a character and tell why they chose their character, describing that character's traits using textual evidence that supports their interpretation. Next, students decorate pumpkins to look like characters from their books. Students describe the theme of the book and create a multimedia visual that depicts the major events of the book, using tools such as Canva or Adobe Spark. To share their book report information with others and to encourage their classmates to read their book, the students use Vimeo or YouTube to host their videos. The teacher will use Flipsnack, a software tool that enables students to create stylish digital flip books, to display all of the videos. The teacher will publish the Flipsnack show in the fourth-grade weekly parent newsletter and on the class Facebook page, as well as show it to the fourth-grade class to celebrate students' learning.

In this redesigned lesson, we have considerably strengthened the Domain Knowledge question in section A of the protocol because we connected it to substantive ELA learning goals. Students now are learning discipline-specific and discipline-relevant knowledge and skills in ELA, whereas the original lesson only asked students to state the name of their character.

When we strengthen one component of the 4 Shifts Protocol, it is fairly typical for several other components to become stronger as well. In this revised lesson, for instance, we have deepened the Critical Thinking question in section A as students describe the traits of their character and find evidence in the text to support those character traits. When teachers ask students to support their claims with evidence, the level of thinking increases. In addition, the students now must create a visual using the major parts of the story and also have to determine their story's theme, which calls for them to engage in more interpretative work than in the original activity.

When the teacher has shared students' recordings via Flipsnack on the class Facebook page and in the fourth-grade weekly parent newsletter, his or her students' work begins to make a contribution to an audience beyond the classroom walls (Authentic Assessment, section B, page 15). We could strengthen this component even further if the teacher shares resultant student work products in an educative way with other students, not just parents (for example, book recommendations to a class in another state or country). Since the students' learning is now public rather than confined to the classroom, students almost inevitably will be more intentional about the quality of their work and what they include and highlight in their videos. The redesign also requires students to explicitly understand character traits generally as well as those of their book character specifically (Assessment Technology, section B). The other assessment element that gains strength in the revision is the Assessment Alignment question in section A. The level of thinking called for by the content standards and learning goals better aligns to the level of thinking in the assessment because teachers ask students to explicitly describe their character with the traits that they identify and support their assertions with evidence from the text. Moreover, students have to determine the theme of the story and then tell a story using appropriate facts and relevant, descriptive details to support that theme, all while speaking clearly and at an understandable pace. Typical fourth-grade ELA standards require these types of learning goals, and this is what the students must do in their videos to demonstrate their learning.

Finally, we will note that we also somewhat strengthen the Communication Technologies question in section D of the protocol in the redesigned lesson because students now are using images to facilitate the communication process when they create a visual using tools such as Canva or Adobe Spark to depict the major events of the story. The students also are recording themselves and then pulling all of the videos together using Flipsnack. The more teachers allow students to do this technological work instead of doing it themselves, the stronger this question becomes.

Elementary School Mathematics

For our third example of lesson or unit redesign, let's visit a sixth-grade mathematics classroom. We're all familiar with story problems to help encourage critical thinking, but let's see how we can use one to deepen student learning even more.

The Treehouse

In this lesson, a teacher assigns the following story problem to her students from their mathematics textbook:

> You have 1,400 square feet of boards to use for a new treehouse. Design a treehouse that has a volume of at least 250 cubic feet. Include sketches of your treehouse. Are your dimensions reasonable? Explain your reasoning.

The Redesign

In this scenario, we like that the story problem asks students to design a treehouse instead of some other structure that they may have never heard of or seen before. Treehouses are structures that many students are familiar with and think would be fun to play in. We also like that students include sketches of their treehouse and have to use mathematical and real-world reasoning to support their sketches. The story problem is a decent start, but we think we can do even better.

We believe that this learning task lends itself to asking students to play the role of a treehouse designer, a person who designs treehouses. You might be curious about how we came up with that role. Well, we just googled, "Who designs treehouses?" When we looked at a few companies' websites, we saw that they describe their employees as designers. We also know that there is even a television show called *Treehouse Masters* that showcases the creation process of treehouse designers as they make treehouse masterpieces. Identifying a role like this helps us design for a student-centered approach to learning. Another added benefit in this case is that students start to become more aware of various occupations that use mathematical concepts and thinking. While examining a few commercial treehouse websites, we also looked at some of the language the sites use in the descriptions of what treehouse designers do. We did so in order to help provide a more realistic feel for how these experts actually use mathematics.

Once we determine that a treehouse designer is a great way to focus the lesson, we can ask ourselves, "For whom might a treehouse designer design treehouses?" We decide that a family in a student's own neighborhood is a suitable audience. Most families have to create and use budgets when engaging in home improvement projects. Having a family as a simulated audience also connects well with the limitations of the original problem—1,400 square feet of boards. After all, the family only can afford so much wood, and the tree is only so big, right?

Another thing that treehouse designers need to consider when designing a treehouse is how much space the family will need for its furnishings and whether any city ordinances or building permit requirements might come into play. This connects back to the volume requirement of 250 cubic feet. A building permit may also limit homeowners when building outdoor structures. Introducing real-world contexts and constraints helps students understand the rationale for why the problem would state such limitations.

After thinking about what a treehouse designer would do and creating some two-dimensional draft sketches of a treehouse, we think the next step in the process might be to have students take their sketches and put them into a 3-D modeling program in order to make the necessary adjustments. Once students finalize their designs, we can have students use the 3-D modeling software to create a model or prototype of the treehouse and print it using a 3-D printer. This would help them avoid wasting building materials and see if their designs actually print to scale without any errors. With these ideas in mind, the task might read something like this:

> You are a treehouse designer and your neighbor would like you to design a treehouse for her children. Your neighbor also wants draft sketches and a 3-D prototype of the treehouse before it is built so that she can better envision the treehouse. This also allows you to make necessary changes without having to start again from scratch and waste building materials. Your neighbor is on a budget and already has purchased the lumber, which consists of 1,400 square feet of boards. Due to the furniture that she plans to use, the neighbor wants the treehouse to have a volume of at least 250 cubic feet. Since the neighbor's budget is pretty tight, a proposal that includes calculations and 3-D modeling sketches is necessary since she also has contacted a competing treehouse designer and wants to go with the best proposal. Using a persuasive presentation, a proposal supported by mathematical concepts and reasoning, and a prototype, can you convince your neighbor to go with your proposal?

If you look at sections A and B of the 4 Shifts Protocol, hopefully you will see that we have strengthened three questions—those for Domain Knowledge, Domain Practices, and Domain Technologies—with this redesign. Instead of simply asking students to complete an isolated story problem, students now must use—in context—important mathematical concepts such as scale, proportion, volume, and other geometric concepts. Students are *using* mathematics instead of just doing mathematics. They are employing both procedural and conceptual mathematics for a purpose: to solve a real problem similar to what contractors, builders, and architects (and, yes, treehouse designers) do in their day-to-day work. Drafting sketches—and designing and creating prototypes and models—are practices and processes that these professionals commonly use when completing their projects. When we couple these robust engineering and design practices with important mathematical concepts, the level of thinking naturally increases. Finally, our philosophy is to always think first about the purpose or function of the learning before we pull in any learning technologies. Now that we are more comfortable with the solidity of the learning and the validity of the mathematical context and functions (compared to the original lesson), we are ready to determine which technologies might make sense. In this redesigned task, discipline-specific technologies include students working with computer-aided design software, 3-D modeling software, and a 3-D printer, which frequently are available in a school's industrial technology area, media center, makerspace, or computer lab.

Other areas of the protocol that we think are stronger after this redesign are the Critical Thinking question in section A and many of the questions in section B. Constrained by the family budget and basic geometry, students must engage in a variety of critical thinking and problem-solving tasks to get to the final product if we design and implement this learning opportunity correctly. As we ask students to do work such as making sketches, transforming those sketches into 3-D drawings, and creating models and prototypes, they are engaging in authentic and meaningful work that reflects the work experts do outside of school. As we strengthen the authenticity and relevancy aspects of a lesson or unit (section B), numerous opportunities to deepen student learning typically emerge. Focusing on sections A and B in the protocol often creates high-leverage approaches to learning. In other words, when we create conditions for students to engage in relevant learning, the level of academic rigor usually increases.

What also makes this a high-leverage redesign is that it asks students to incorporate some ELA skills. Originally just a mathematics problem from a textbook, it now has an interdisciplinary component from another core area. Students now must also create an informative technical proposal—including all plans, prototypes, and mathematical calculations—and a persuasive presentation in order to convince the neighbor to go with their ideas. These are examples of authentic, literacy-related products and performances. Accordingly, students probably will put more time and effort into their products, which should result in higher-quality student work. You get bonus points if you can move this task beyond a simulation, get a builder in the community to judge the proposals, have the winning design result in an actual treehouse for someone in the community, and display students' entries in a space that the public frequently visits!

We hope that you're starting to get an idea of how the 4 Shifts Protocol can help educators redesign lessons and units for technology integration. Now that we've covered several elementary school examples, in the next chapter we will do the same for middle and high school examples.

Chapter 4

Redesigning Secondary Lessons and Units

In this chapter, we present three examples that show how educators might use the protocol for secondary lesson and unit redesign. The previous chapter includes three elementary school redesign examples. The next chapter contains one elementary and one secondary unit that we designed from the beginning with the protocol. Once again, we strongly encourage you to read every chapter, even if it doesn't address your grade level or subject area, to see what ideas may transfer into your own instructional work.

High School Life Science

For our fourth example of lesson or unit redesign, let's visit a tenth-grade science classroom. In this class, the teacher gives her students a few weeks to work on a project about bacteria, and they show their learning by creating posters.

Bacteria Poster

In this unit, each student creates a poster about a water-borne bacterium that can be harmful to humans, the bacterium's effects, and disease prevention and treatment (see Larmer & Mergendoller, 2010). The teacher then displays the best posters in the hallway.

The Redesign

In this scenario, we like that the teacher intends students to do some kind of project and that the activity involves them learning about water-borne bacteria that can be harmful to humans. The teacher has placed at least a small emphasis here on learning that goes beyond a worksheet or review questions. Also, the teacher attempts to address a current real-world issue.

We're going to take the original idea and redesign it into a performance task. A performance task is an activity that engages students to apply their learning and develop a product, performance, or both. A performance task can be both a rich learning experience and an assessment.

When designing a performance task, we like to start by identifying a role that the students might play (similar to the treehouse scenario in chapter 3, page 27). This helps frame the performance task and provides students with the opportunity to act as if they are experts outside of school. The Authentic Role question in section B (page 14) of the 4 Shifts Protocol connects very nicely with this idea. When we put students in an authentic role, we often have the ability to leverage the actual practices, processes, and domain-relevant technologies that people in those disciplines use to do their work efficiently and effectively. So we can start by thinking about who in the real world works with water-borne bacteria. Some potential roles might be a conservationist, an environmentalist, a water-quality technician, or a biologist. For this example, we like the idea of having students act in the role of environmentalists.

Now that we have identified the authentic role, the next thing that we need to determine is the authentic audience. The easiest way to think of the audience is to put it in the form of a question: "Whom does the environmentalist need to inform?" In this case, the student environmentalists would need to inform the citizens in their area so that the local community knows the adverse effects of water-borne bacteria and what could prevent and treat this potential danger. Finally—and only now in the design process—do we determine what authentic products or performances the students as conservationists could create for the citizens in your area. There are numerous answers to the question, "What might be the best ways to inform citizens?" Possible answers might include displays at the library, presentations to the city council or local businesses, informational fliers at public events, student-created brochures at local businesses, public service announcements on the local radio station, and letters to the editor in area or state newspapers.

Now that we have determined a role, audience, and a few potential products or performances, the task might read something like this:

> You are an environmentalist. You have been asked to inform citizens of your county [list your county] about a water-borne bacterium in the nearby river [name the river], including its effects, prevention, and treatment. Choose one of the following presentation formats so that we may inform citizens of [list your county] of the effects, prevention, and treatment of water-borne bacteria. Let's try to have a variety of presentation and information-sharing formats so that we reach as many people as possible.

In this revised scenario, note that we have strengthened section B, Authentic Work, of the protocol because students now are thinking and working in the roles of environmentalists. Their research work now has a larger purpose, which hopefully will help drive student motivation and engagement. If there are water-quality issues in the area and students actually inform citizens in the county of effects, prevention, and treatment, then the contribution to an outside audience is a meaningful component as well. In the original scenario, students only are involved in some very basic research and only a few get to passively present their information in class to their teacher and their classmates. Although the posters in the hallway are intended to highlight student learning excellence, other students and visitors may not pay much attention to the shared information.

In this revised task, note also that the Technology as Means, Not End question in section D (page 17) is in play because instructional purpose now drives any technologies that the lesson uses and the use of those tools is embedded within authentic work. Students can use a variety of technologies to create their work products, including word processing or podcasting software, video cameras, graphic design and infographic tools, slideware, and so on, and they could ground all of it in the needs of their particular audiences. The Technology Adds Value question in section D also becomes stronger as the authenticity increases. In fact, for many of the student work products and authentic audiences, it would be very difficult to communicate the necessary information without using task-specific technologies. Relevant and robust uses of technology send a message to students and the community that digital tools are vital contributors to powerful knowledge work. Similarly, the Authentic Assessment question in section B becomes richer as students work with real-world audiences in mind.

One bonus of this particular redesign is that it asks students to incorporate a variety of ELA skills into the work. Originally just a science lesson, it now has an interdisciplinary component. Asking students to create information products such as op-ed letters, public service announcement storyboards, or podcasting scripts allows them to create authentic, literacy-related work products. Students probably will need to put more time and effort into their products and—as in the Flipsnack shown in chapter 3—the end results should be of higher quality because students know that outside community members are going to be looking at and judging what they make.

Middle School Health

For our fifth example of lesson or unit redesign, let's look at a middle school health lesson. One traditional lesson is to ask students to imagine that they are food traveling through the digestive system. Some teachers use a Food Postcards activity to conduct this lesson.

Food Postcards

In this lesson, teachers give students the task of creating a series of postcards to describe a trip through the digestive system. More specifically, students select a particular food and then create five postcards that they compose from that food item's point of view. On one side of each postcard, students draw a picture of something the food might "see" on its journey. On the other side of each postcard, students write a description of the events the food experiences. For example, suppose the food a student chooses is an apple. The postcard describing the mouth might have a picture of teeth on the front. The message on the back might begin, "Dear Mac, so far I have had a miserable trip. I haven't even left the mouth yet, and already the teeth that you see on the other side of this postcard have torn me apart, crushed me, and cut me into pieces."

For this lesson, teachers expect students to include the structures and functions of the digestive system that they describe and define any health terms that they use in their descriptions. Students' first postcards feature the mouth, and students should mention the role of the teeth in mechanical digestion and the role of saliva in chemical digestion. Students' second postcards relate to the food's journey through the esophagus. Students should describe how the body keeps food from entering the windpipe and how mucus and peristalsis help to move the food through the esophagus. The third postcards cover the stomach and should describe both mechanical digestion by the contraction of muscles and chemical digestion by digestive juices. The fourth postcards feature the small intestine. For these cards, students should describe the chemical digestion that occurs as a result of the enzymes and secretions of the small intestine, liver, and pancreas. They also should discuss how nutrients are absorbed through villi. The final postcards come from the large intestine. Students should mention the bacteria that feed on the material passing through the large intestine. They also should note that water is absorbed into the bloodstream and that the rest of the material is eliminated. Throughout the postcard creation process, students should try to include as much information about the digestive system on their postcards as they can.

The Redesign

This lesson has quite a few positives. First, we really like how the teacher provides some agency to students by letting them choose the type of food. We also like how the food takes on a persona, as this could allow students to be creative. Another aspect of the lesson that appears to be fairly strong is that students must include the structures and functions of the digestive system as the food travels through the digestive system and, in doing so, they describe and define any science terms.

On the surface, this lesson seems to take on a nuance that many other lessons don't have. Typical digestive system lessons would include drawing the human body and labeling the parts, including arrows showing how food enters and exits the body. While this lesson appears to have some potential for higher-order thinking because students take on the perspective of food traveling through the digestive system, in actuality it is lower-order thinking because it predominantly asks students to engage in description. Notice that the activity is heavily directed by the teacher, including very tight expectations for what students must include on each postcard.

As we think about how we could rebuild this lesson to support the task's original intent, we believe that it makes sense to keep the perspective of the food traveling through the digestive system. When students think about something through a different lens, teachers can unlock many interesting possibilities for higher-level thinking. Let's hang on to that idea. To capitalize on this opportunity to allow students to be creative and drive their own learning, we would make this more open-ended and let students choose how they want to show their understanding of the digestive system.

When we look for what the lesson asks students to know, do, and understand, it appears that the heart of the lesson gets lost when students draw pictures and describe the events that the foods experience. Unfortunately, the specific directions from the teacher overshadow students' thinking. To match the intended purpose of the lesson with the enacted purpose, we can instead ask students to explain the structures and functions of the digestive system—addressing the concepts of absorption, elimination, and digestion—and include the specific health vocabulary that they previously discussed and learned throughout their digestive system unit. As reconfigured, the lesson could read something like this:

> Imagine that you are a food traveling through the digestive system. How can you describe its trip? You will select a particular food and choose how you want to illustrate how your food travels through the digestive system. You could have your food take a trip and use postcards, write and read a poem, compose and sing a rap, write and act out a skit, take a series of social media photographs with captions, use a sports analogy, or use technologies such as Chatterpix or Blabberize (which are great tools to show perspective), using your food as the object.

> If you have another idea, let's talk about it together. The main learning that you need to show is your explanation of your food's point of view as it travels through the digestive system, starting with the mouth and ending with the large intestine. During your food's journey through the digestive system, you must provide an explanation of the structures and functions of the digestive system, addressing the concepts of

> absorption, elimination, and digestion, including the specific health vocabulary words that you previously learned throughout the digestive system unit.

Notice that in this revised scenario, we have attempted to make the lesson stronger using section A of the 4 Shifts Protocol. Notice also that some of the redesign options allow students to still engage in deeper thinking but don't require technology tools at all (and that's okay). When students look at the gastrointestinal journey from the food's point of view, they have to determine what specifically happens to their food as it travels through the organs of the digestive system and also use the appropriate health terms in their explanation. Not only do students have to more deeply understand functions such as absorption, elimination, and digestion, they also have to understand what makes up the food and how the body converts those components into energy and basic nutrients as they pass through the organs. This isn't anything that students would be readily able to simply reproduce.

In this revised activity, note that we have strengthened the Creativity question in section A of the protocol. Instead of confining students to the teacher's designated end product, they now have the opportunity to be creative by designing their own way to illustrate how their chosen food travels through the digestive system.

As we think about other protocol connections, we think that the Domain Knowledge question in section A (page 13) is now stronger as well. With the revised lesson we can see that students are now learning discipline-specific knowledge and skills connected to big, important health and science concepts: absorption, elimination, and digestion. Some of this shift happened when we took away the teacher-prescribed steps for the postcards and instead focused on the important conceptual learning. Additionally, we strengthened section C (page 15) of the protocol, particularly the Assessment of Learning and Technology Selection questions. Instead of requiring all students to use postcards to describe the food's trip through the digestive system, students now have a choice and are able to select how they would like to demonstrate their understanding of the important concepts. Similarly, students now have more agency regarding the technologies that they would like to use in their end product. They could use technologies such as stop motion, Chatterpix, or Blabberize to show perspective; make videos; create a simulated Instagram account; or use a whole host of other self-selected technology tools.

High School Physical Science

For our sixth lesson redesign example, let's look at a high school science teacher's attempt to have students take good notes and learn about sedimentary rock.

Sedimentary Rock

In physical science, ninth-grade students use a teacher-provided Google Doc to fill in blanks while they listen to the teacher share information about sedimentary rock using an interactive, multimedia Prezi slide deck. Students then submit their copy of the document back to the teacher using Google Classroom so that she can assess note-taking accuracy and whether students were paying attention.

The Redesign

In this not-so-complex scenario, we like that the teacher strives for student engagement. We also think that using the visual effects of the Prezi slide deck might be an attempt to try something novel and mix things up a bit so that students pay attention and retain the information. However, the level of cognitive demand for students in this activity is fairly low, as are the usages of technology by both the students and the teacher.

We think that there is an opportunity here to open this lesson up and give students some flexibility in the direction that they want to take their learning. In order to do so, it is helpful to know what the learning goal and important concepts are for students so that they have a focus for their discovery and findings. In this particular scenario, the students are supposed to understand and apply their knowledge of the structures of the Earth system and of the processes that change the Earth and its surface.

In the original lesson, the teacher does not ask students to understand or apply their understanding of the Earth system or of the processes that change the Earth and its surface. One strategy to make this more open-ended would be to turn the learning goal into an essential question by using a *how* or *why* question stem. These types of open-ended questions can give students opportunities to research some possible answers while simultaneously allowing the teacher to provide guidance throughout student exploration. Another part to this strategy is to refine students' discovery processes by asking probing questions that require students to begin to make connections to the real world. While students are searching for answers, the teacher can ask them additional real-world questions. If framed adequately, we think that students could get excited about their learning as they research these questions and begin to discuss their findings with their teacher and classmates, generating additional questions until eventually they decide what information they want to share and with whom they would like to share it. Eventually, the redesigned lesson might read something like this:

> As ninth-grade students, your challenge is to use one or both of the following essential questions to guide your research and demonstrate your understanding and application of the structures and processes of the Earth system and the processes that change the Earth and its surface.

- How do the structures and processes of the Earth system change the Earth and its surface?

- Why do processes such as plate tectonics and national disasters change the Earth and its surface?

After doing your initial research, use some of the following questions to refine your research and determine who would benefit from your findings and whether you should take an informative or persuasive approach.

- What are the implications for cities, seaports, and countries when these structures and processes change the earth and its surface?

- What examples, past and present, are there of these events?

- What should we start or stop doing and why?

- Who needs to be informed or persuaded about these issues?

Based on these decisions, determine the best format for your presentation and deliver a presentation about your findings to an authentic audience. Remember to consider the most appropriate technologies that will assist you as you research, create your presentation, and share your findings to that outside audience.

Notice that in this revised scenario we have changed the focus of students' learning so that it is centered more around big, important concepts in earth science: the structure and processes of the earth system. Altering the fact-based sedimentary rock lesson to an activity that focuses more on earth science concepts; providing an open-ended, inquiry-based approach to student learning; and asking students to construct their own knowledge using information literacy strategies in the research process all strengthen the Domain Knowledge and Deeper Learning questions in section A of the 4 Shifts Protocol.

When a lesson is focused around big, important themes and concepts (section A of the protocol), we often see opportunities to also increase the authenticity and relevance of a lesson (section B). We find this to be true in this scenario. Because students are researching real-world issues and presenting information about those issues—including warnings and potential solutions—to authentic audiences, this should feel more like real work rather than fake work. We also strengthen the Contribution subquestion in section B when we ask students to share their findings with someone who would benefit from their research.

In this revised version of the lesson, a few questions in the Student Agency and Personalization area (section C) of the protocol also are more robust, including Learning Activity, Work Time, and Initiative. For instance, the selection of how students learn the material is now a partnership between the teacher and the students: the teacher provides guiding questions that lead students toward the learning goal and students have the freedom to choose the lines of inquiry that interest them. While students are working on answering those essential questions through an inquiry-based process, the Research and Information Literacy Strategies question in section B has now shifted. Students also get some say regarding how they will demonstrate and apply their learning—either by informing or persuading an audience of their choosing—so the Assessment of Learning question (section C) gets a small boost. Additionally, the teacher encourages students to select technologies that will help them research efficiently and effectively, create their presentation, and share their findings with an appropriate audience.

The lesson redesign strengthens student agency. The two questions in section C that shift the most are probably Talk Time and Work Time. Instead of sitting, listening, and following along fairly passively within an activity that is heavily teacher-directed, students now are the primary drivers of their learning because they are doing the majority of the talking and working, using essential questions and extension questions from the teacher to guide their learning process. The teacher moves from a "sage on the stage" role to that of a facilitator of learning, even though the learning goal remains the same. In regard to the Technology Usage question in section C, the answer to "Who is the primary user of the technology?" shifts from a fairly uninspiring *both*—teacher as lecturer, students as notetakers—to *students* as they take on more responsibility for decision-making and information-generating. In the revised lesson, there is no mention of which technologies the students are supposed to use. In fact, at first glance, we have subtracted technology from the lesson as the teacher is no longer imparting information with Prezi and the students are no longer taking notes with Google Docs. As teachers expose their students to many different technologies, connect them to specific functions or purposes, and ask them to take greater ownership of those decisions, students eventually build capacity, become more independent, and are able to choose the right tools and technologies for the job.

We encourage teachers to design or redesign lessons and units so that they ask students to think at a conceptual level rather than at topical or factual levels. When that happens, many things change for the better within classrooms, including greater student meaning-making and engagement. If students are thinking and working with important themes and concepts rather than just listening and taking notes, it is much easier to provide opportunities for deeper thinking, relevance, and transformative technology use. In the next chapter, we shift our attention from redesigning existing lessons and units to designing new ones.

Chapter 5

Designing From Standards

So far we have provided six examples of how the 4 Shifts Protocol (page 13) can help educators redesign existing lessons, and we encourage you to read through all of them to see what ideas may transfer into your own classrooms. In this chapter, we illustrate how teachers also can use the protocol to design lessons or units from scratch, using examples from elementary school social studies and high school English language arts. For this design process to succeed, we believe that it is critical to start with a rich, deep, robust content standard. This standard should be conceptual in nature, ask learners to construct knowledge, and encourage authentic or highly relevant student work. This work would reflect that of experts outside of school and students would most likely share it to an outside audience.

Elementary School Social Studies

In the first of our two original design examples, we are going to use a second-grade social studies standard to launch a new unit.

Promoting Change or the Status Quo

Let's consider a learning standard that would ask students to understand that individuals and groups within a society may promote change or the status quo. We can see numerous possibilities in this standard and feel that it meets the criteria of being rich, deep, and robust. The relevance or real-world component of the standard comes from the opportunity for students to research how individuals and groups have promoted change or the status quo in the past and how they also are doing so in the present. Once students have made sense of who has done this and how, we can ask them to think of something that they would like to do as an individual or in a group that would promote change or the status quo. Turning this standard into an action item for students allows them to engage in authentic work similar to that done by people outside of school.

The Design

Now that we have a standard that can launch the unit, let's see how we can take our understanding of the 4 Shifts Protocol from the previous redesign examples and use that understanding to design from the beginning. In order for students to begin to understand what they need to learn and how they are to demonstrate that learning, the students could read about various activists during whole- and small-group instruction. As they read, they should identify main ideas with supporting details and then use this information to discuss how that individual promoted change. This helps level the playing field for students who may be unaware of important activists and sets everyone up for future success. Then, it's time to brainstorm. Students could use digital graphic organizers such as Popplet (http://popplet.com), Bubbl.us (https://bubbl.us), Padlet (https://padlet.com), or Kidspiration (www.inspiration .com/Kidspiration) to identify other individuals or groups—past or present—who have promoted change or the status quo (and what they promoted). These individuals and groups may be famous or historical figures or might even be local people whom the students know personally. Students' ideas can come from something that they previously read or viewed, something that they learned about in a social studies or science lesson, personal interactions and experiences, or other prior knowledge.

Once they have completed this initial brainstorming activity, students choose an individual or group that they would like to research. As part of that research, students would need to find out and report on whether the individual promoted change or the status quo as well as why and how he or she did so. Students would gather and organize this information, using a graphic organizer and word processing software throughout the process. After students have collected their information, they can decide how to share it with their classmates. Among many possibilities, students could make a multimedia presentation, create an infographic, or write an informative piece in which to share their findings.

Once students have shared their research with their peers, they can deepen their understanding of the standard and demonstrate their learning by investigating how they themselves can promote change or the status quo. Such an action project can begin with students thinking about rules that they want changed or talking to people in their families, schools, and communities about problems, issues, and concerns that they are facing. After they have done some initial interviews and have determined what challenge they want to pursue, the students can begin mind mapping and brainstorming plans for addressing the issue or concern. For students who might struggle with this aspect, teachers can provide them with question prompts to help spur their thinking. For instance, the teacher can ask them if there is a rule that they don't agree with in the lunchroom, on the playground, in the classroom, at home, or in their neighborhood and if they have some good reasons why the rule should be changed. Students can then use the same graphic organizer tools to help gather and organize their information while they do research to support their claims. Finally, students can share their findings with an appropriate, authentic audience that the students' arguments could possibly influence. The newly designed unit overview might read something like this:

> During whole-group instruction, second-grade students read and learn about an activist who has stood up for change. Students will have opportunities to ask and answer questions about the text as well as identify the main ideas and supporting details. Next, during small-group instruction, the students receive explicit reading instruction with the teacher when reading books about other activists such as Rosa Parks, Leonard Crow Dog, Rachel Carson, and Cesar Chavez. While some students are with their teacher during small-group instruction, the other students pair up with a partner and take turns reading paragraphs from other books highlighting the work of different activists. As they read, they should identify main ideas with the supporting details and then use this information to discuss how that individual promoted change. After these initial activities, students will use graphic organizer tools such as Popplet, Bubbl.us, Padlet, or Kidspiration to identify other individuals or groups, past or present, who have promoted change or the status quo and what they promoted. From this brainstormed list, students will select an individual or group to research. They will use a graphic organizer and word processing software to organize the information that they find about why their individual or group promoted change or the status quo, the successes that they experienced, and the challenges that they faced and overcame. Students will choose a presentation technology to share their findings. Finally, either as an individual or in groups of two or three, students will interview people in their homes, schools, and communities to identify unaddressed problems, issues, or concerns in a local setting. Students will decide how they plan to promote change or the status quo and then do the research necessary to convince an audience of their choosing either to do nothing or to make the change for which the students are asking. In their final product or performance— using appropriate technologies to support a letter to the editor, public service announcement, podcast, or multimedia presentation—students attempt to persuade their authentic audience about what change should be made (or not) and why and who would benefit from their proposal.

Numerous components from the 4 Shifts Protocol are evident in the new unit. We start with the Deeper Learning question in section A about whether student work focuses on big, important themes and concepts by designing the unit around the big, important social studies concept of change versus the status quo. We provide an open-ended, inquiry-based approach to learning and have students construct their own knowledge using information literacy strategies (section B, page 15) as part of their research. Students engage in Critical Thinking and complex, messy Problem Solving (section A, page 13) both when they interview people and investigate what issues, problems, or concerns are in their homes, schools, and communities and when they research evidence to bolster their claims and attempt to convince a relevant audience to support their position.

Throughout the unit, students have a great deal of agency (section C, page 15) since they are the primary drivers of both the talk time and work time. We also think that the Interest-Based and Initiative questions in section C are in play because students can choose an area of interest or passion when determining how they, as individuals or groups, would promote change or the status quo. Within this work, students are able to be entrepreneurial, self-directed, and go beyond the basic learning task and take it in directions that they desire. Students are the primary users of the technology both when they brainstorm and research and when they develop their final product or performance. They also are the ones who select which technologies they use in their work (Technology Selection, section C), although the teacher might suggest a few options. Additionally, students have a lot of choice in the Assessment of Learning question (section C) about how to demonstrate their knowledge and skills for this social studies standard as they think about their intended audiences and how to best convey their persuasive messages.

As students begin to move their work from the classroom to an outside audience, that work shifts toward greater relevance and authenticity (Authentic Assessment and Contribution, section B). Now, instead of simply sharing ideas with the teacher and some classmates, the second graders are attempting to make a difference in their school or community through persuasive argument. As such, they begin to make contributions beyond their classroom walls to the world around them.

One bonus of this newly designed unit is that it asks students to incorporate a variety of ELA and 21st century skills (Partnership for 21st Century Learning, 2018) into the work (similar to the bacteria poster in chapter 4). While we began with a single social studies standard to launch the design of this unit, it now has strong interdisciplinary components. Students are interviewing people in the community, conducting research to find evidence to support their opinion, organizing information in a way that is usable and helpful, synthesizing information, and creating persuasive products or performances such as letters to the editor, public service announcements, podcasts, infographics, and multimedia presentations. All of this allows students to create authentic literacy-related work products and performances.

Notice how the technologies we mention in this scenario align to function or purpose. There is very little focus on the technologies themselves as an end goal.

They always are a means to something larger and more important. Even though the teacher might suggest some technologies, the unit allows for a great deal of student autonomy. Digital technologies add value to students' work but hopefully never overshadow, mask, or otherwise draw the focus away from important learning (Technology as Means, Not End, section D, page 17).

High School English Language Arts

In the previous section, we showed you how to design a new elementary social studies unit rather than redesigning an existing one. In the second of our two original design examples, we illustrate what a similar process might look like in a high school ELA classroom, using informative text.

Informative Text

For this unit we are going to use an ELA standard for grades 9 and 10 about writing to inform. The standard asks students to write informative and explanatory texts to "examine and convey complex ideas, concepts, and information clearly and accurately through the effective selection, organization, and analysis of content" (W.9–10.2; National Governors Association Center for Best Practices & Council of Chief State School Officers, 2010). In this design example, we will focus on just the informative side of the standard. We can see some rich possibilities since this standard appears to demand action and calls for higher-order thinking. As in the previous example, we believe that this standard is an excellent opportunity for students to identify a real-world issue about which they are passionate and then—as the standard demands—write to inform by conveying complex ideas and information clearly and accurately to authentic audiences.

The Design

Let's see how we can set students up for success before we launch the unit. We think that students can do some initial informative writing on a topic that is relevant to them, such as a current topic at school, in the community, or in the news. Teachers can use this piece of writing as a preassessment to determine what students already know and can do and to identify what assistance students might need as they work toward their end products. Students also can look at a mentor text in order to inform their own understanding. They can dissect the mentor text together—using a teacher-provided, standards-aligned rubric—in order to identify and comprehend the components of a high-quality, informative piece of writing, focusing particularly on task, purpose, and audience. Using the results of these warm-up activities, students receive teacher guidance toward—or request to participate in—side seminars designed to help them with areas in which they have low confidence or need assistance. Putting students in the driver's seat regarding their own writing supports can help them own their learning in ways that teacher-directed interventions may not.

Now that we've identified a rich, robust, and deep content standard that we can build on and also some initial warm-up activities to help inform necessary student supports, we are ready to design additional activities in the unit. The plan is to ask students to identify an issue that they are highly interested in or passionate about, with the end goal of informing an authentic audience who cares about that topic. Numerous online resources are available to help students identify potential topics, including TweenTribune (www.tweentribune.com), Google News Archive (http://news.google.com/newspapers), Newsela (https://newsela.com), DOGO News (www.dogonews.com), and the National Writing Project's Youth Voices website (http://nycwritingproject.org/youth-voices). Teachers can even configure some of these resources to their students' reading levels. We also can help students connect to ideas they have discussed in other classes, in their extracurricular organizations, or in outside organizations or activities that they are involved in through their faith institutions, homes, neighborhoods, or workplaces. For example, if students also were in an industrial technology class, they could use this writing exercise to create technical reports, specification papers, or proposals. Similarly, if they were simultaneously in a social studies or science class, students could narrate historical events, scientific procedures or experiments, or technical processes. With some teacher coordination, students could receive credit for satisfying both ELA standards and standards in other disciplines.

Once they determine their topics, students can use advanced graphic organizer tools such as Lucidchart (www.lucidchart.com), MindMeister (www.mindmeister.com), Google Drawings (https://docs.google.com/drawings), or Google Docs (www.google.com/docs) to help organize their facts, details, and examples as they conduct their research and prepare their arguments. Google Docs can be helpful for writing drafts and sharing with others in order to receive feedback from classmates, the teacher, and possibly also outside experts who are knowledgeable about the chosen topic. The needs of students' authentic audiences and perhaps the conventions of the discipline will determine the format of their writing. For example, if the authentic audience is an advisory board, the writing may need to be in the form of a technical report or a policy proposal, along with an accompanying slide deck. Other possibilities might include a letter to the editor, a YouTube video, a public service announcement, an infographic, a spoken word performance, or a podcast.

Once students have identified the audience and format, they can reconfigure their initial research and writing to ensure that it is appropriate for their needs. If the actual writing the standard calls for isn't obvious in a particular product or performance, students can use their structured prewriting and other developmental activities as evidence of meeting the standard (for example, they might show the screenplay for a video or the slide notes for a voice-narrated slide deck). As they work on their final products, students should determine the technologies that are most appropriate for the task and audience. Some of these technologies might include Microsoft Word or Google Docs, PowerPoint or Keynote, Adobe Photoshop or InDesign, Piktochart, Audacity, Scrivener, GarageBand, Clips, or iMovie. Once their end products are ready, students should actually share their information with the intended audience. Afterward, students can respond to some reflective, open-ended questions to help them think about what they did, how they did it, how well they did it, and what they would do differently next time in order to learn from the experience and apply it to future activities.

Ultimately, the newly designed unit overview might look something like this:

> Ninth- or tenth-grade students will identify an issue or topic that they are highly interested in or passionate about with the end goal of writing to inform an authentic audience. The issue or topic may be related to what is occurring or under discussion in their classes, extracurricular activities and organizations, homes, faith institutions, workplaces, community, state, nation, or world. Students also may use a variety of online resources to identify potential topics. During the research stage, students will use graphic organizers, mind-mapping software, word processors, and other technologies to help organize their facts, details, and examples. They will use Google Docs to write and share an initial draft of their informative piece and receive feedback from others (including, perhaps, outside experts). Students will take their draft writing and reconfigure it into the most appropriate format for their audience and discipline. Possible formats might include policy proposals, letters to the editor, technical reports, multimedia presentations, YouTube videos, public service announcements, infographics, podcasts, and more. Students will utilize appropriate information and communication technologies to share their end products with their intended audiences. Finally, students will reflect on what went well and what they would do differently next time.

This unit is similar in many ways to the elementary social studies unit that we discuss earlier in this chapter. Although the student writing here is informative rather than persuasive, it also is aimed at outside, authentic audiences and features many of the same writing strategies and techniques. Like the elementary social studies project, this unit provides an opportunity to connect very nicely with other disciplines and includes several additional 21st century skills and ELA standards—creativity, critical thinking, reading, researching, language, and speaking and listening—that teachers can address.

In this scenario, the Domain Knowledge and Deeper Learning questions of the 4 Shifts Protocol (section A) should be very strong since we designed the unit from the beginning around a rich, deep, robust content standard. The standard for writing to inform asks students to construct knowledge and implicitly to produce work that reflects that of experts in the outside world. Right from the start we can see that students are learning discipline-specific and discipline-relevant knowledge, skills, and dispositions and that their work focuses on big, important concepts central to ELA. When students are writing to inform their authentic audiences, they are using the same research, inquiry, and information literacy strategies (Research and Information Literacy Strategies, section B) that writers use. As students use graphic organizers and other writing tools and technologies to organize their thinking, construct and synthesize their knowledge, and format their end products, they are employing the same practices, processes, and tools (Domain Practices and Domain Technologies, section B) that writers and multimedia content creators use from beginning to end. Moreover, since students are creating technical reports, policy proposals, public service announcements, videos, and other informative products and then sharing them with authentic audiences, they more than satisfy the Real or Fake, Authentic Assessment, and Contribution questions in section B of the protocol.

Throughout this lesson, students should be involved in learning activities that allow them to engage in critical thinking and complex problem solving (section A). With relatively little guidance, they have to create complex end products that convey detailed and technical information to authentic audiences. As they engage in that work, they have the opportunity to design, create, make, or otherwise add value that is unique to them when they choose their topic, write their informative piece, and put it into a format that makes sense for their audience (Creativity, section A). They receive a lot of creative freedom within this lesson. At the end, teachers also ask students to engage in metacognition (section A), the opportunity to reflect on their planning, thinking, work, and progress.

Although students receive the learning task based on the standard for writing to inform, they have a great deal of flexibility on how to acquire the desired knowledge and skills (Learning Activity, section C). For instance, they can request a seminar to get assistance on a writing skill or concept for which they have low confidence, or they can be very independent and just complete the work. Students also have significant autonomy to determine how they demonstrate what they know and can do and which technologies they use along the way (Assessment of Learning and Technology Selection, section C).

What we perhaps like best about this activity is that it involves a significant amount of student agency (section C). Students are central in their own learning from the beginning to the end. Although the teacher provides a few parameters, students drive the topic choice, the audience and technology selection, and the format and sharing of the end product. Throughout the process, students are the ones doing the majority of the talking, thinking, and working. They choose topics that reflect their own interests and have multiple opportunities to initiate, manage their own work, and be entrepreneurial.

Section D of the protocol (Communication and Communication Technologies) comes into play at several stages of the process, first when students are receiving feedback on their drafts and later when they are sharing with others. Throughout the writing and sharing processes, students are using information and communication technologies in appropriate, meaningful, and relevant ways, ensuring that the digital tools are adding value and providing a means to larger, more important ends (Technology Adds Value and Technology as Means, Not End, section D).

Finally, we believe that this activity richly represents the Assessment Alignment component in section A of the protocol. Student assessment should align cognitively with standards, learning goals, instruction, and learning activities.

So far we have redesigned a few lessons and units for elementary, middle, and high schools. We also have designed a couple units from scratch using learning standards and the protocol. In our final chapter, we offer some general tips, strategies, and other suggestions for using the 4 Shifts Protocol to enhance technology integration in your schools and classrooms.

Chapter 6
Implementing the Protocol—Techniques, Strategies, and Suggestions

In the preceding chapters, we provide some examples of lesson and unit (re)design to give you an idea of how schools and educators can use the 4 Shifts Protocol to move instructional activities toward deeper thinking and learning, authentic work, student agency and personalization, and technology infusion. As we note at the end of chapter 2, we have found few books that offer concrete suggestions regarding lesson and unit redesign. Hopefully, you found our examples both informative and inspiring. This is complex instructional work! If we can help our fellow educators think more deeply and critically about *instructional purpose* when we pull technology tools into students' learning work, we can use the protocol to assess whether we are accomplishing those goals *and* to pivot in desired directions if our answers aren't yet what we want them to be.

As you think about using the 4 Shifts Protocol in your own classrooms and school buildings, consider the following techniques, strategies, and other suggestions that we have compiled from our own usage of the protocol.

Intentional Design

These kinds of instructional (re)design conversations often are not easy, but they are important. If we have larger system-level goals around deeper learning, greater student agency, more authentic work, and rich technology infusion, we have to redesign our day-to-day instruction to get us there. We also have to provide adequate supports (see, for example, the International Society for Technology in

Education's [2018a] *Essential Conditions*). Inserting technology into our classrooms and hoping that magic will happen are not enough.

Structure Versus Winging It

If we ask teachers, instructional coaches, technology integrationists, or principals how to (re)design a technology-infused lesson or unit, most of the time they respond that they just kind of wing it. Neither of the dominant technology integration frameworks—SAMR and TPACK—provide enough detail to think through what to include or change in a learning activity, so people decide fairly idiosyncratically what to focus on and which tools to use. As a result, most technology usage in schools is fairly low level, predominantly teacher-centered, and highly variable across classrooms. We intentionally designed the 4 Shifts Protocol (page 13) to add structure to educators' technology integration conversations and to give them some concrete look-fors and think-abouts to align with instructional purposes that go beyond replication, regurgitation, and recall. We have found that the concreteness of the protocol questions is far more helpful to most teachers than the general categories of the SAMR and TPACK frameworks. Accordingly, the protocol seems to be a good complement to these frameworks: as educators start shifting their lessons using the protocol, they almost inevitably start moving up the SAMR ladder or closer to the center of the TPACK diagram.

A Set of Experiences Over Time

The entire 4 Shifts Protocol can be pretty overwhelming. *Select only a few* sections or bullet points to address at any given time. When picking a section, consider starting with section A (specifically the Domain Knowledge and Deeper Learning questions), which many educators have found to be a high-leverage section. Technology integration always should be purposeful and targeted. Hopefully, students will get to live in all of these areas multiple times over the course of a school year (mix it up!) but for any given lesson or activity, target just a few. The goal is not to hit every aspect of the protocol every time for every lesson, unit, or activity. A more reasonable goal is for students to have opportunities to experience each of the areas in the protocol multiple times over an academic year, hopefully in combination.

Professional Learning and Expectations

Do we want students to have multiple opportunities to engage in deeper thinking over the course of a school year? Yes, probably. Do we want students to have multiple opportunities to do authentic, real-world work over the course of a school year? Yes, probably. Do we want students to have multiple opportunities in a school year to have some agency, control, and ownership over their own learning? To engage in rich, technology-infused communication and collaboration experiences? Yes, probably.

If we think of the protocol sections as sets of experiences that we want students to have over the course of an academic year, we probably should consider how to design curriculum, professional development, and expectation mechanisms to make sure this happens. Some schools take one individual section of the protocol at a time and dedicate several professional learning sessions to help teachers succeed with that section. Then on to another one . . . .

Mindset Shifts

In addition to shifting our instruction and our support structures, we also have to shift our thinking. The biggest barriers to making the 4 Shifts are our deeply embedded mindsets and belief systems about what schools should look like and how they should operate.

Critical Interrogation

We have to be willing to set our egos aside and ask thoughtful, often challenging questions about whether or not learning technologies are accomplishing deeper learning purposes in our classrooms or are merely replicating traditional factual recall and procedural regurgitation. In other words, we must be willing to *critically interrogate* both our instructional intent and the accompanying usage of technology in our classrooms. If we don't have the will to self-examine and change what we do, the results of our technology integration efforts will be lackluster.

We use the hashtag *#makeitbetter* to represent the idea that—if we're willing to put everything back on the table for reconsideration, including our possibly fragile psyches—there is always room to make something better, no matter how good the original lesson or unit is. We want the word *amazing* to describe what happens with students in our classrooms. Don't you?

The Power of the Pivot

If you like the answers that you're getting to the protocol questions, then awesome, keep doing that! Otherwise, use those same questions to help you execute a redesign pivot. Focus on desired answers to the question, If we wanted the answer to the question to be this instead of that, how could we redesign the lesson, activity, or unit differently to get there? Do this collaboratively with others to diversify experience and expertise and to optimize idea generation.

Avoidance of Judgment

Focus on brainstorming, idea generation, dialogue, and problem solving, not judgment or evaluation. We actually don't care which level of SAMR you're on (particularly since the lines between them are so blurry). We have no need to label or judge you. We are interested, however, in what your reasons are for pulling technology into your lessons or units and whether or not you're successfully accomplishing those purposes. If you're achieving what you wish, great. If not, let's use the protocol to help you get there.

The 4 Shifts Protocol should never function as a "gotcha" mechanism that administrators or peer reviewers use to evaluate teachers. The last thing we want is for classroom observers to run down the protocol x-ing boxes and saying, "Nope, nope, nope," because a teacher is rightfully and thoughtfully focusing on just a few of the questions.

Growth and Change Over Time

One of the strengths of the protocol is that it allows for movement by all teachers, regardless of their starting points or comfort levels. Some educators will be ready to take a set of questions in the protocol and run far with their (re)design. Others will need to take smaller steps with that same section. Either way, the educators are moving in necessary and desired directions and we should honor and celebrate both of those journeys. Focus on growth over time. Allow teachers to choose which sections and bullet points they work on. Pick small areas in which to shift, plant some seeds, watch them grow, build upon the successes, and learn from the inevitable failures (but don't give up!).

Student Involvement

Your students can help with this. Even younger students can help (re)design lessons and units (really!). Ask students questions like, "Here's how this has been done in the past. If we wanted it to be this instead, what could that look like? How could we get there? What ideas do you have for making this more interesting and more awesome?" Students' answers are almost invariably insightful. We just have to be willing to give up a little control and treat students as co-owners of their learning experience.

Protocol Implementation With Fellow Educators

When we introduce the 4 Shifts Protocol to educators, we never start with their own lessons or units. We reduce reflexive defensiveness by using the protocol with instructional activities that aren't theirs. The videos and lesson plans from the Arizona and Florida Technology Integration Matrices (Arizona K12 Center, 2012;

Florida Center for Instructional Technology, 2011) can be good places to start. We will pick several lessons from those websites that are as close as possible to those of the group we're working with (for example, if it's a group of middle school educators, we will use middle school lessons). We then take a single lesson and practice answering questions from one protocol section at a time, making sure that we are on the same page about what we see. Then, we will ask educators to use a couple of questions from that same section to redesign the lesson and make it better. Then, we move on to a new lesson and a new section. After several rounds, folks usually are familiar and comfortable with the basic ideas behind and usages of the protocol. The crosswalk available at the 4 Shifts resources page (bit.ly/4shifts) can help you identify which lessons might be good to use with particular protocol sections.

Some principals and instructional coaches don't introduce the 4 Shifts Protocol to their educators at all. They don't want it to be another thing on educators' already overflowing plates. Instead, they just start using the protocol to ask better questions when they talk with teachers. Someday they will inform the teachers of where the questions are coming from and help them build their capacity to use the protocol themselves. But not this year . . . .

Use of the Protocol

Teachers, principals, instructional coaches, and technology integrationists can use the 4 Shifts Protocol in a variety of ways. For instance, the protocol might be a helpful planning tool for lesson study, within the professional learning communities (PLCs) process, and in other settings in which educators are creating and implementing lessons collaboratively. Using the protocol as part of learning walks might be another way; principals and other teachers could look for evidence of implementation, focusing on a few sections that a colleague decided to work on. Teachers and other education leaders could use the protocol by focusing on a few areas that connect to the current professional learning in their building or district or by diagnosing existing lessons and units and striving for alignment with larger school mission and vision statements, desired learning outcomes, and other organizational goals. Higher education faculty can introduce the protocol to their preservice educators as a design tool for moving student learning activities toward deeper thinking and learning, student agency and personalization, authentic work, and technology infusion. The possibilities are endless.

Be creative and share with us how you're using the protocol!

The 4 Shifts Protocol Versus Project-Based Learning (PBL)

We are big fans of project-, inquiry-, and challenge-based learning. If you have the inclination and capacity in your school and classrooms to do that complex learning work, by all means do so! We have found, however, that a space seems to exist between most educators' current instructional practice and full-blown PBL. Many teachers find that the planning and instructional demands of full-scale, "gold-standard" PBL (Larmer & Mergendoller, 2015) are too daunting for them at the current moment. Nonetheless, there are smaller shifts that educators can make in their instructional activities that enable deeper thinking and learning, authentic work, student agency and personalization, and technology infusion while they work toward more complex projects. The 4 Shifts Protocol can be helpful for educators who want to start shifting their instruction but aren't ready yet for large-scale PBL work. Over time, these shifts add up, can have big impacts on school learning cultures and climates, and can help educators proceed toward even more complex instructional work.

The 4 Shifts Protocol Is a Creative Commons Document

We have released the 4 Shifts Protocol with a Creative Commons Attribution-NonCommercial-ShareAlike 4.0 International copyright license. The protocol is already in use by thousands of educators all around the world. Feel free to use part or all of it in any way that makes sense to you. Make it work for you and your context and please share with us how you are using the questions. If you might benefit financially from those uses, please contact us first and let us know what you are considering. If you have suggestions for improvement, let us know those too so that we can consider them for the next version. Help us make the protocol better!

Epilogue
Staying in Touch

We hope this book and the redesign examples that we included have been useful to you. We always are delighted to chat about harnessing technology for deeper learning. Both of us talk and work with educators and school systems on a daily basis. Please don't hesitate to get in touch and let us know how we can support you. We look forward to hearing from you about your journey!

- Scott McLeod, dr.scott.mcleod@gmail.com, @mcleod, http://dangerouslyirrelevant.org

- Julie Graber, jckgraber@gmail.com, @jgraber

Visit **bit.ly/4shifts** for other 4 Shifts Protocol resources.
#4shifts #makeitbetter

References and Resources

Archambault, L. M., & Barnett, J. H. (2016). Revisiting technological pedagogical content knowledge: Exploring the TPACK framework. *Computers and Education, 55*(4), 1656–1662.

Arizona K12 Center. (2012). *Arizona technology integration matrix.* Accessed at www .azk12.org/tim on May 17, 2018.

Azzam, A. M. (2007). Special report: Why students drop out. *Educational Leadership, 64*(7), 91–93. Accessed at www.ascd.org/publications/educational-leadership /apr07/vol64/num07/Why-Students-Drop-Out.aspx on January 23, 2015.

Bagshaw, E. (2016, April 1). "The reality is that technology is doing more harm than good in our schools" says education chief. *The Sydney Morning Herald.* Accessed at www.smh.com.au/national/education/the-reality-is-that-technology-is-doing -more-harm-than-good-in-our-schools-says-education-chief-20160330-gnu370 .html on May 17, 2018.

Barnwell, P. (2016, April 27). Do smartphones have a place in the classroom? *The Atlantic.* Accessed at www.theatlantic.com/education/archive/2016/04/do -smartphones-have-a-place-in-the-classroom/480231 on May 17, 2018.

Bauerlein, M. (2008). *The dumbest generation: How the digital age stupefies young Americans and jeopardizes our future (or, don't trust anyone under 30).* New York: Penguin.

Bloom, B. S. (Ed.), Engelhart, M. D., Furst, E. J., Hill, W. H., & Krathwohl, D. R. (1956). *Taxonomy of educational objectives: The classification of educational goals— Handbook 1: Cognitive domain.* New York: David McKay.

Bray, B., & McClaskey, K. (2014). *Updated personalization vs. differentiation vs. individualization chart version 3.* Accessed at www.personalizelearning. com/2013/03/new-personalization-vs-differentiation.html on July 1, 2018.

Bugeja, M. (2005). *Interpersonal divide: The search for community in a technological age.* Oxford, England: Oxford University Press.

Busteed, B. (2013, January 7). *The school cliff: Student engagement drops with each school year* [Blog post]. Accessed at www.gallup.com/opinion/gallup/170525 /school-cliff-student-engagement-drops-school-year.aspx on October 10, 2014.

Carr, N. (2010). *The shallows: What the internet is doing to our brains.* New York: Norton.

Center for Authentic Intellectual Work. (2018). *AIW framework.* Accessed at www .centerforaiw.com/aiw-framework on July 1, 2018.

Cuban, L. (2001). *Oversold and underused: Computers in the classroom.* Cambridge, MA: Harvard University Press.

Cuban, L. (2016, January 30). *Kludge: A metaphor for technology use in schools* [Blog post]. Accessed at https://larrycuban.wordpress.com/2016/01/30/kludge-a -metaphor-for-technology-use-in-schools on May 17, 2018.

Florida Center for Instructional Technology. (2011). *The technology integration matrix.* Accessed at http://fcit.usf.edu/matrix/matrix on May 18, 2017.

Guo, J. (2016, May 16). Why smart kids shouldn't use laptops in class. *The Washington Post.* Accessed at www.washingtonpost.com/news/wonk/wp/2016/05/16/why -smart-kids-shouldnt-use-laptops-in-class on May 17, 2018.

Hamilton, J. (2008, October 9). *Multitasking teens may be muddling their brains.* Accessed at www.npr.org/templates/story/story.php?storyId=95524385 on May 17, 2018.

Harris, J., & Hofer, M. (2009). *Welcome to the learning activity types (LATs) website.* Accessed at http://activitytypes.wm.edu on May 17, 2018.

Hughes, J., Thomas, R., & Scharber, C. (2006). Assessing technology integration: The RAT—replacement, amplification, and transformation—framework. In C. Crawford, R. Carlsen, K. McFerrin, J. Price, R. Weber, & D. Willis (Eds.), *Proceedings of the Society for Information Technology & Teacher Education International Conference 2006* (pp. 1616–1620). Chesapeake, VA: Association for the Advancement of Computing in Education.

International Society for Technology in Education. (2018a). *Essential conditions.* Accessed at www.iste.org/standards/essential-conditions on July 1, 2018.

International Society for Technology in Education. (2018b). *ISTE standards.* Accessed at www.iste.org/standards on July 1, 2018.

Iowa Core. (2010). *Iowa core standards.* Accessed at https://iowacore.gov on July 1, 2018.

Iowa Core. (2018). *Characteristics of effective instruction.* Accessed at https://iowacore .gov/content/characteristics-effective-instruction-0 on July 1, 2018.

Keen, A. (2007). *The cult of the amateur: How blogs, MySpace, YouTube, and the rest of today's user-generated media are destroying our economy, our culture, and our values.* New York: Doubleday.

Kessler, A., Phillips, M., Koehler, M., Mishra, P., Rosenberg, J., Schmidt-Crawford, D., et al. (2017). The technological pedagogical content knowledge (TPACK) framework: Lineages of the first ten years of research—Part 1. In P. Resta & S. Smith (Eds.), *Proceedings of Society for Information Technology and Teacher Education International Conference* (pp. 2376–2380). Accessed at www .learntechlib.org/primary/p/177532 on June 29, 2018.

Koehler, M. (2012). *Using the TPACK image.* Accessed at http://matt-koehler.com /tpack2/using-the-tpack-image on August 27, 2018.

Krathwohl, D. R. (2002). A revision of Bloom's taxonomy: An overview. *Theory Into Practice, 41*(4), 212–218.

Lanier, J. (2010). *You are not a gadget: A manifesto.* New York: Knopf.

Larmer, J., & Mergendoller, J. R. (2010, September). Seven essentials for project-based learning. *Educational Leadership, 68*(1), 34–37.

Larmer, J., & Mergendoller, J. R. (2015, April 21). *Gold standard PBL: Essential project design elements* [Blog post] . Accessed at www.bie.org/blog/gold_standard _pbl_essential_project_design_elements on May 17, 2018.

McLeod, S. (2014, December 22). We need schools to be different. *The Huffington Post.* Accessed at www.huffingtonpost.com/scott-mcleod/we-need-schools-to-be -dif_b_6353198.html on June 28, 2016.

McTighe, J., & Wiggins, G. (2013). *Essential questions: Opening doors to student understanding.* Alexandria, VA: Association for Supervision and Curriculum Development.

Microsoft. (2018). *Skype in the classroom.* Accessed at https://education.microsoft .com/skype-in-the-classroom/overview on July 1, 2018.

Mishra, P., & Koehler, M. J. (2006). Technological pedagogical content knowledge: A framework for teacher knowledge. *Teachers College Record, 108*(6), 1017–1054.

National Council of Teachers of English. (2017). *NCTE 21st century literacies framework.* Accessed at www.ncte.org/digital-literacy on July 1, 2018.

National Governors Association Center for Best Practices & Council of Chief State School Officers. (2010). *Common Core State Standards for English language arts and literacy in history/social studies, science, and technical subjects.* Washington, DC: Authors. Accessed at www.corestandards.org/assets/CCSSI_ELA%20Standards .pdf on May 24, 2017.

Oppenheimer, T. (2010, February). *Multitasking mentality.* Accessed at www.pbs
.org/wgbh/pages/frontline/digitalnation/living-faster/split-focus/multitasking
-mentality.html?play on May 17, 2018.

Partnership for 21st Century Learning. (2017). *Skills for today research series.* Accessed
at www.p21.org/our-work/4cs-research-series on July 1, 2018.

Partnership for 21st Century Learning. (2018). *Framework for 21st century learning.*
Accessed at www.p21.org/our-work/p21-framework on July 1, 2018.

Porter, B. (2010). *Technology and learning spectrum.* Accessed at https://go.shr
.lc/2zb0GO6 on July 1, 2018.

Puentedura, R. R. (2006). *Transformation, technology, and education.* Accessed at
http://hippasus.com/resources/tte/part1.html on May 17, 2018.

Richtel, M. (2010, June 6). Attached to technology and paying a price. *The New York
Times.* Accessed at www.nytimes.com/2010/06/07/technology/07brain.html on
May 18, 2018.

Rockmore, D. (2014, June 6). The case for banning laptops in the classroom. *The New
Yorker.* Accessed at www.newyorker.com/tech/elements/the-case-for-banning
-laptops-in-the-classroom on May 17, 2018.

Shirky, C. (2014, September 8). *Why I just asked my students to put their laptops away.*
Accessed at https://medium.com/@cshirky/why-i-just-asked-my-students-to-put
-their-laptops-away-7f5f7c50f368 on May 17, 2018.

Shulman, L. S. (1986). Those who understand: Knowledge growth in teaching.
Educational Researcher, 15(2), 4–14.

Shulman, L. S. (1987). Knowledge and teaching: Foundations of the new reform.
Harvard Educational Review, 57(1), 1–22.

Stiggins, R. J., Arter, J., Chappuis, J., & Chappuis, S. (2012). *Classroom assessment for
student learning: Doing it right—Using it well* (2nd ed.). Upper Saddle River, NJ:
Pearson.

Turkle, S. (2011). *Alone together: Why we expect more from technology and less from each
other.* New York: Basic Books.

Valentine, J. (2018). *Instructional practices inventory.* Accessed at www
.ipistudentengagement.com/ipi-process-in-depth/overview-of-ipi-process on July
1, 2018.

Wagner, T. (2008). *The global achievement gap.* New York: Basic Books.

Webb, N. L. (2002, March 28). *Depth-of-knowledge levels for four content areas.*
Accessed at http://facstaff.wcer.wisc.edu/normw/All%20content%20areas%20
%20DOK%20levels%2032802.pdf on July 1, 2018.

Wiggins, G., & McTighe, J. (2005). *Understanding by design* (2nd ed.). Alexandria, VA: Association for Supervision and Curriculum Development.

Solutions for Creating the Learning Spaces Students Deserve

Solutions Series: Solutions for Creating the Learning Spaces Students Deserve **reimagines the norms defining K–12 education. In a short, reader-friendly format, these books challenge traditional thinking about schooling and encourage readers to question their beliefs about what real teaching and learning look like in action.**

Creating a Culture of Feedback
William M. Ferriter and Paul J. Cancellieri
BKF731

Embracing a Culture of Joy
Dean Shareski
BKF730

Making Learning Flow
John Spencer
BKF733

Reimagining Literacy Through Global Collaboration
Pernille Ripp
BKF732

Different Schools for a Different World
Scott McLeod and Dean Shareski
BKF729

Personalizing Learning Through Voice and Choice
Adam Garry, Amos Fodchuck, and Lauren Hobbs
BKF657